GOD'S ORDER
THE EPHESIAN LETTER AND THIS PRESENT TIME

BY JOHN A. MACKAY

A PREFACE TO CHRISTIAN THEOLOGY
CHRISTIANITY ON THE FRONTIER
GOD'S ORDER:
The Ephesian Letter and This Present Time

GOD'S ORDER

THE EPHESIAN LETTER AND THIS PRESENT TIME

by

JOHN A. MACKAY

*President of Princeton Theological Seminary
Princeton, N.J.*

WIPF & STOCK · Eugene, Oregon

Wipf and Stock Publishers
199 W 8th Ave, Suite 3
Eugene, OR 97401

God's Order
The Ephesian Letter and this Present Time
By Mackay, John A.
Copyright © 1953 by Mackay, John A. All rights reserved.
Literary Agent - John Mackay Metzger
Softcover ISBN-13: 979-8-3852-3299-4
Hardcover ISBN-13: 979-8-3852-3300-7
eBook ISBN-13: 979-8-3852-3301-4
Publication date 9/13/2024
Previously published by The Macmillan Company, 1953

This edition is a scanned facsimile of the original edition published in 1953.

To Sherwood and Elena Reisner in the patio of whose home among the mountains of Mexico most of this book was written.

Prologue

This Book and Its Theme

The Book

This book contains the substance of the Croall Lectures which it was the author's privilege to deliver in the University of Edinburgh, in the month of January, 1948.

The original invitation to give the Croall Lectures came to me in 1938 during the principalship of that distinguished churchman and scholar, now retired, the Rev. William A. Curtis, D.D. The Lectures were to have been delivered sometime in 1941. In the meantime, the Second World War broke out. Apart from the difficulties of trans-Atlantic travel, commitments to Princeton Theological Seminary and to the Church at large, arising out of the new situation created by the War, brought about the postponement of the Lectures. During the intervening years more than one theme was proposed to the Trustees of the Croall Lectureship, and accepted by them, only to be changed again.

But at length the subject was chosen which forms the title of this volume. It grew upon me that nothing would be more relevant to the contemporary situation in the Church and in the world, especially in view of the approaching organization of a World Council of Churches in Amsterdam, than a discussion of the Epistle to the Ephesians. The fact that the original phrasing of the Amsterdam Assembly theme had been changed from "The Order of God and the Disorder of Man" to "Man's Disorder and God's Design," without, in my judgment, any justifiable reason for the change, made me the more determined to retain in the title of the Edinburgh lectures the word "order," which I regarded irreplaceable if the idea underlying it was to be truly conveyed.

On several previous occasions I had dealt with the Ephesian Letter. At one of the early sessions of the Princeton Institute of Theology, later at Montreat in the mountains of North Carolina, and at Massanetta Springs in the valley of Virginia, thoughts on a favorite theme were presented in a somewhat informal and fragmentary way. But as I looked forward to the honor, dear to every Scotsman's heart, to lecture in the capital city of the land of his fathers, and within the precincts of a school of Divinity, rich in theological tradition, which is now part of Edinburgh University, I set myself to give more developed form to musings that had engaged my mind for many years.

Four years have passed since the Lectures were delivered. Their preparation for publication encountered difficulties, the difficulties which confront every administrator in the ecumenical era. At length, during a sabbatical leave among the mountains of Northern Mexico, for which I am indebted to the Trustees of Princeton Theological Seminary, I was able to get ready the major part of the manuscript for the press. Two years later it was finally completed during a brief sojourn in Texas.

I take this opportunity to express my very deep appreciation to the members of the Croall Trust for their unfailing courtesy and boundless patience in those years when the theme of the Lectures was being changed and the date of their delivery was being constantly postponed. They would have been entirely justified in cancelling the Lecture contract. That they did not do so makes them co-partners in the production of this volume which, but for their gracious forbearance, might never have seen the light. Let them, and, with them, Principal Hugh Watt now retired, and his successor, Principal John Baillie, and the Faculty of New College, accept my deep gratitude for an inspiring and unforgettable experience in the Winter of 1948.

The Theme

This book deals with what is called *God's Order*. By God's Order is meant the essential structure of spiritual reality, which has its source in God and whose development is determined by the will of God.

This structure was envisaged most perfectly by St. Paul, through the illumination of the Holy Spirit, in the Epistle to the Ephesians, the greatest and maturest of all his writings. The Structure or "Order" thus envisaged has its center in Jesus Christ. Christ constitutes its core. The development of this structure holds the promise and sets the task of the future, not only the future of human history, but the future of cosmic history as well. The clear discernment of this "Order of God," and the loyal fulfillment of its claims, are of first rate importance for Christianity and civilization in our time.

But in our study of the Ephesian Letter it is no futuristic Utopia that will concern us. We shall not be dealing with some dream of what *might be*, nor yet with some ideal way of thought or life which *should be*. What will engage our thoughts is something that now *is* in essential, nuclear form. God's Order actually *exists*, however imperfectly, in the Christian Church, which God has designed to be the true integrating center and pattern for human life and relations. This "Order," as outlined in the inspired vision of St. Paul, will achieve its ultimate dimension through what he describes "as a plan for the fullness of time, to unite all things in Him [that is, in Christ], things in heaven and things on earth" (Eph. 1:10). The development and triumph of this Order are embraced in, and guaranteed by, the eternal Purpose of God. Through the study of what Paul calls the "mystery," the "open secret of God," and its implications for human life, we are helped to make sense of the world in which we live, to focus with clarity its essential problems, and to envisage God's solution for its sin and His divine pattern for its life.

In preparing this volume, I have done my best to become acquainted with the best existing studies on St. Paul and the Epistle to the Ephesians, and to make them tributary to an exposition of the greatest, and for our time, the most relevant of his works. Yet this book does not aim to be a commentary on Ephesians in the ordinary, traditional sense. It aims to be less and also to be more than this. Omitting the minutiae of exegetical erudition, but taking into account everything in the Letter that is essential for the understanding of Paul's thought, the present volume is concerned simply and exclusively with the core and central doctrines of this most important of Christian documents, and with their bearing upon the human situation today.

JOHN A. MACKAY

Princeton, New Jersey
May 1952

Contents

Prologue — vii
   This Book and Its Theme — vii

1. PERSPECTIVES — 1
   a. Apostolic Proclamation — 1
   b. A Lyrical Interlude on Biblical Authority — 4
   c. A Letter, Pauline and Ecumenical — 10
   d. A Compendium of Christian Truth — 14
   e. Doctrine Set to Music — 17
   f. The Most Contemporary Book in the Bible — 19

2. THE GREAT RIFT — 25
   a. The Transcendental Rift — 26
   b. The Historical Rift — 35
   c. Human Approaches to the Rift — 43

3. GOD'S UNVEILED SECRET — 51
   a. Its Apostolic Medium — 51
   b. Divine Overture — 53
   c. The "Mystery of His Will" — 59
   d. Love Everlasting and Invincible — 64
   e. The Historical Organ of an Eternal Purpose — 68

4. THE VICTORY WHICH CHRIST WROUGHT — 73
   a. Faith's Core and Clue: A Person — 73
   b. A Life Destined for Death — 75
   c. Through Crucifixion Conquest — 83
   d. Exaltation — 91

5. NEW MEN IN CHRIST — 96
   a. "In Christ" — 97
   b. Men in Christ — 99
   c. By Grace — 103

CONTENTS

    d. Through Faith — 105
    e. Unto Peace — 112
    f. For "Good Works" in the Church's Service — 116

6. THE NEW DIVINE ORDER — 122
    a. The "Church Which Is His Body" — 123
    b. Images of the Church — 129
    c. The Great Unities — 135

7. THE FULLNESS OF CHRIST — 145
    a. Out of His Fullness—Gifted Men — 145
    b. Towards His Fullness—An Effective Ministry — 149
    c. The Realization of His Fullness—Christian Maturity — 158

8. THE FOUR IMPERATIVES OF CHRISTIAN LIVING — 165
    a. Walk in the Light — 167
    b. Copy God — 169
    c. Learn Christ — 172
    d. Be Filled with the Spirit — 176

9. CHRISTIAN ACTION ON THE FRONTIERS OF STRIFE — 184
    a. The Frontiers of the Natural Order — 187
        The Principle of Christian Action: "In the Lord" — 187
        Action on the Domestic Frontier — 188
        Action on the Business Frontier — 191
    b. The Frontiers of the Supernatural Order — 195
        The Panoply of God — 196

Epilogue — 201
    Courage, Therefore! — 201

Appendix — 203
    The Letter of Paul to the Ephesians — 203

Index — 211

GOD'S ORDER
THE EPHESIAN LETTER
AND THIS PRESENT TIME

CHAPTER I

Perspectives

Before we look into the Ephesian Letter, let us look at it. Before listening in detail to what the book says, let us learn some things about the book itself. Let us in a word seek to attain that kind of perspective which is indispensable when we engage in the study of ideas and their significance.

a) APOSTOLIC PROCLAMATION

The theme of the Ephesian Letter is, as I stated in the Prologue, God's Order. This order, it is important to observe, Paul *proclaims*. He does not reason about it in discursive thought, nor envision it in poetic image. In making the proclamation, Paul, the author of this document, speaks like a herald, and not like a philosopher or poet. His heraldic proclamation of something which God had revealed to him puts the substance of his thought outside the more usual categories of speculative idea and mythological symbol.

There is every evidence in the life and writings of St. Paul that he was interested in philosophy and that he was acquainted with the philosophy of his time. But his description of the Order of God was not a composite picture based upon first principles and elemental truths which he had discovered in a study of nature, man or history, and then arranged in a logical system under the inspiration of a central luminous idea. That was how Plato organized his famous "Republic." Paul, however, makes it perfectly clear that the sublime structure which he was setting forth was not a product of human speculation at its best, nor was it in any sense a creation of man's wisdom. He attributed his insight into the "mystery" of God's purpose in constituting this supreme spiritual reality as due to the action of God Himself, who was pleased to reveal the matter to him.

Nor was Paul's view of this divine order what is ordinarily described as poetic vision. In the apprehension of spiritual reality the poets have always been more penetrating and creative than the philosophers. To the poets we owe our understanding of the fact that all true interpretation of reality, human or divine, must be based upon a grasp of the essential image which provides the light in which things must be studied and the form in relation to which they can be understood. This image is what is commonly called "myth," when "myth" is used in the poetic or philosophic sense, to signify the image of an ultimate truth, and not in the unfortunate popular sense, as the synonym for a shameless fiction. It was the great merit of the poet, William Blake, that he saw with great clarity that the supreme task of the true poet is to envision and interpret the essential image. This essential image, or "myth," cannot be presented in conceptual, but only in pictorial form, often in the form of a story. When Plato was confronted with the necessity of presenting truths which, on account of their transcendental character, could not be stated in conceptual terms, he told stories. These stories are the Platonic myths. When the prophets of Israel and the seer in the Apocalypse wished to set forth things which human "eye hath not seen nor ear heard," things which had not entered into human experience, they wrote in highly pictorial and symbolic language.

But St. Paul in presenting the Order of God goes beyond poetry and apocalyptic in the same way that he goes beyond philosophy. He had all "that haunting awareness of transcendental forces peering through the cracks of the visible universe," which for some is the very essence of myth.[1] He was clearly aware of the problem of communication which has led to the contemporary definition of myth as "a large controlling image that gives philosophical meaning to the facts of ordinary life." [2] He would be ready to admit that without such images "experience is chaotic, fragmentary and merely phenomenal." [3] When Paul, however, envisioned the supreme spiritual structure of reality and announced that Jesus Christ was the "Head of His Body the Church," a society which God had constituted to be the pattern for true human unity and the seat of the power which alone could produce unity; and when he went on to say that God had designed a much vaster unity in which He would "sum up" in Christ things terrestrial and things celestial, he was proclaiming what, according to his own deep conviction, had been unveiled to him by God Himself as the core of all reality and the clue to all understanding of reality.

Paul the Apostle, in his heraldic proclamation of the Order of God, stands thus in a place by himself, beyond philosopher and poet, beyond prophet and seer. What comes to us through him is neither a reasoned conclusion nor a mythological interpretation; it is not merely prophetic insight into the foundation of the moral order nor a reassuring affirmation of the victory of God in history. Here we have rather the supreme and concrete de-

---

[1] Philip Wheelwright, quoted by Mark Schorer in *William Blake: The Politics of Vision*, p. 28.
[2] Mark Schorer in *Id.*, p. 27. [3] *Id.*

scription of what is involved in the creed of the Apostolic age, which is the basic creed for every age, namely, that *Jesus Christ is Lord* (Phil. 2:11).

b) A LYRICAL INTERLUDE ON BIBLICAL AUTHORITY

At this point the question may properly be raised, Why should we take St. Paul and the Ephesian Letter seriously? Why should we regard the content of this first century document as the ultimate unveiling of the purposes of Deity, both of what God has done and of what He intends to do? The answer to this question is: Because the Epistle to the Ephesians occupies a central part in a book, the Bible, which the Christian Church believes to be the record of God's self-disclosure to mankind.

This brings up the question of Biblical authority, a question which I wish to consider before going any further with this discussion. What right do we have to attach to the Bible, or to any part of the Bible, the kind of authority which is here attributed to it? What ground is there for the assumption that we find in the Bible an authoritative revelation of God and a description of the ultimate structure of spiritual reality? With what reason can it be maintained that in the Bible and only in the Bible we are brought face to face with God's self-disclosure of Himself and His will?

One thing is certain. The Bible cannot be appreciated or understood by people who approach it with an air, and in the spirit, of pure objectivity. The person who comes to the Bible merely to look at it, to examine its truths with a cold scrutiny, bringing to bear upon his study all the apparatus of research and the encyclopedic knowledge of human documents, but without personal commitment to the God whom the Bible reveals, will utterly fail to understand or appreciate the Book. The reason is obvious. After the Biblical text and the thought therein enshrined have been most carefully explored from the viewpoint of language and historical background, after the life and ideas of the

Biblical personalities have been studied, the main import of the Bible's significance and message remains untouched. The Bible demands that those who study it should become willing to adopt the basic attitude towards God and life which it challenges men to adopt. It demands especially that they submit to the sway of that central Figure, Jesus Christ, whom it presents. When men are willing to adopt a Biblical point of view, to put themselves in the perspective from which the Bible looks at all things and to identify themselves with the spiritual order of life which the Bible unveils, they understand the Bible, they see those spiritual realities about which the Bible speaks. If the unique self-disclosure of God and His will are to make any sense, if they are to make a true impression upon the student of the Biblical records, "eyes of faith" are needed.

This is the method which the Bible itself proposes for validating the truth it proclaims. Obedience to God is the prerequisite for insight into God. Only when the spectator becomes a wayfarer upon the highway of God's purposes, only when he is willing to identify himself with God's great scheme of things as it is revealed in the Bible, is he capacitated to understand the Bible way of looking at things. In a word, when the detached observer of things Biblical becomes an actor in the Biblical drama, when he begins to think with the Bible and not simply about the Bible, when he follows the road signs that lead him to certain hills of vision, then and only then can he believe with all his heart that he has been listening to the Eternal. Then he will behold things that are veiled from scientific objectivity, he will follow in the footprints of the saints, he will become a citizen of the Commonwealth of God. For the Bible is validated, as every ultimate truth contained in the Bible is validated, by an inner witness in the human student of the Bible, the witness of the same Holy Spirit to whose special illumination the writers of the Bible owed their insight into God, His purposes and His works. We cannot get beyond that great, simple affirmation of Thomas à Kempis, that "the Bible is to be read with the same Spirit with which it was written."

But then what becomes of "scientific objectivity"? What about the affirmation that no approach to truth is valid that is not made in "the antiseptic air of objectivity"? In this antiseptic sunlight, it is claimed, all germs die that make objective study difficult: germs of emotion, germs of prejudice, germs of commitment. The answer is that in that kind of approach to truth in which the very existence of the enquirer is at stake no such objectivity can exist. Where ultimate values are involved which must be chosen or rejected, and when one's very life is staked upon their rejection or choice, the whole study is lifted far above and beyond "the antiseptic air of objectivity." When a man's very existence is involved in the particular value that he chooses or the ultimate decision which he makes, there simply is no such thing as absolute objectivity. Vital choices and decisions are made not upon objective, but upon very subjective grounds. When a man's all is at stake, he is obliged to think "existentially." In the realm of personal relations and of ultimate spiritual attitudes existential thinking is the only true and adequate form of thinking. A terrible and inescapable choice confronts every person who would explore the meaning of Biblical truth.

At this point it is difficult to avoid becoming lyrical. That kind of objectivity which some would advocate in the study of religion is for this writer utterly impossible, so far as the Epistle to the Ephesians is concerned. For to this book I owe my life. I was a lad of only fourteen years of age when, in the pages of the Ephesian Letter, I saw a new world. I found a world there which had features similar to a world that had been formed within me. After a period of anguished yearning, during which I prayed to God each night the simple words "Lord, help me," something happened. After passionately desiring that I might cross the frontier into a new order of life which I had read about, which I had seen in others whom I admired, I was admitted in an inexplicable way, but to my unutterable joy, into a new dimension of existence. What had happened to me? Everything was new. Someone had come to my soul. I had a new outlook, new experiences, new attitudes to other people. I loved God. Jesus Christ became the center of everything. The only explanation I could give to myself and to others was in the words of the Ephesian Letter, whose cadences began to sound within me, and whose truth my own new thoughts and feelings seemed to validate. My life began to be set to the music of that passage which begins, "And you hath he quickened, who were dead in trespasses and sins" (2:1).

I had been "quickened"; I was really alive. The quickening came on this wise. It was a Saturday, towards noon, in the month of July of 1903. The "preparation" service of an old-time Scottish Communion season was being held in the open air among the hills, in the Highland parish of Rogart, in Sutherlandshire. A minister was preaching from a wooden pulpit, traditionally called "the tent," to some hundreds of people seated on benches and on the ground, in the shade of some large trees, in the glen. I cannot recall anything that the minister said. But something, someone, said within me with overwhelming power that I, too, must preach, that I must stand where that man stood. The thought amazed me, for I had other plans.

For the rest of the summer I literally lived in the pages of a little New Testament which I had bought for a British penny. Strangely enough, it was the Letters of Paul, rather than the Gospels, which I read and marked most. It was perhaps because the Gospels had been very familiar to me, whereas Paul's Letters, which had never particularly interested me, had for me now in my new outlook all the novelty and freshness of a romance. This was particularly true of the Epistle to the Ephesians which became then, and has continued to be since, my favorite book in the Bible. From the first my imagination began to glow with the cosmic significance of Jesus Christ. It was the cosmic Christ that fascinated me, the living Lord Jesus Christ who was the center of a great drama of unity, in which everything in Heaven and on earth was to become one in him. I did not understand what it all meant, but the tendency to think everything in terms of Jesus Christ and a longing to contribute to a unity in Christ became the passion of my life. It became natural then, and it has remained natural ever since, to say "Lord Jesus," to a personal Presence.

I say this because I want to make perfectly clear that where the Bible, and especially Paul's Letter to the Ephesians, is concerned, I cannot meet the standards of so-called scientific objectivity. Apart from the experience that came to me through the Bible and the vision that met me in the Epistle to the Ephesians, I am nothing, and my life has no meaning. I must be pardoned if I insist, and stake everything upon the insistence, that there is a realm in which, in the deepest sense, subjectivity is truth.

But does this mean that there is no place in the thought and life of a Christian where subjectivity and objectivity can meet? Is there no objective evidence in personal life and providential happenings which can give the sanction of objectivity to something that happened in the inwardness of the soul?

Sometime ago, as I was getting ready for the Croall Lectures in Edinburgh, I opened the pages of an old diary which I kept as a student in Aberdeen, and which I had not looked at for more than thirty years. I found that on February 5, 1908, I had made an entry in which the Rogart experience is referred to.

An adolescent of eighteen, in my first year in college, I was accustomed, as part of my daily devotions, to set down some observations on the Bible passage read. After transcribing the words: "This is a faithful saying, and worthy of all acceptation, that Christ Jesus came into the world to save sinners; *of whom I am chief*" (1 Tim. 1:15), I made this observation: "As I read this chapter and seek to follow the thought of the Apostle a certain sublime cadence seems to fall upon my ear, notes that awaken responsive echoes in the depths of my soul. What is the cause?

Paul obtained mercy. Paul was put into the ministry. Paul was greatly blessed of God. *I*—oh, here I cast my soul on Thee anew —obtained mercy. I obtained a promise to preach the gospel. And, O, my Lord and my Redeemer, do Thou water *my* labors and give increase to the seeds *I* sow. 'Not for my sake, but for Thy own Name's sake.' Deepen my experience. Grant that with the Apostle I may often break forth upon what I owe Thy grace—the chief of sinners and the chief of saviours in the arms of love, and the stars in their midnight courses witnessing to an everlasting betrothal amid the solitude of rugged rocks. Oh, Rogart, my heart yearns for that sweetness again which it enjoyed with its Saviour in thy dear heathered hills. Never, never can I forget thee." The reference to an "everlasting betrothal" may betray the mood of adolescence, and the influence of mystical literature in the evangelical tradition in which I had begun to steep myself. But the memory remains indelible of a passionate protestation to Jesus Christ among the rocks in the starlight, the night following my first deep awareness of the reality of God, that I belonged to Him and that He belonged to me.

Fifty years almost have passed since that boyish rapture in the Highland hills and forty-five since I recalled the experience in a student's lodging in the Granite City. The sun of life is westering, and this mortal pilgrimage must, in the nature of things, be entering the last lap before sunset. Life has been throughout an adventure, a movement from one frontier to another. For me, as I reflect upon the passage of the years, both as regards the authority of the Bible and the meaning of my own life, subjectivity and objectivity can never be separated. A subjective fact, an experience of quickening by God's Holy Spirit in the classical tradition of Christian conversion, moulded my being in such a way that I began to live in Christ and for Christ, and "for His Body's sake which is the Church." My personal interest in God's Order began when the only way in which life could make sense to me was upon the basis of an inner certainty that I myself, through the operation of a power which the Ephesian Letter taught me to call "grace," had become part of that Order, and that I must henceforth devote my energies to its unfolding and fulfillment. The only way in which life makes sense to me now, in the objective realm of history, derives from this conviction: that the Christian Church which confesses her Lord and strives after unity in Him, which unity becomes manifest today as the most universal and the most beneficent reality in history, is itself the core and the true pattern of God's Order in this world, and the promise and pledge of the final consummation of all things in Christ in the world which is to come.

c) A LETTER, PAULINE AND ECUMENICAL

With these preliminary considerations, let us proceed forthwith to get the Ephesian Letter into perspective for intimate study by first examining its origin and nature, and its unique character among writings Biblical and contemporary.

The *author* of this Biblical document, in which the nature of God's Order is more fully unveiled than anywhere else in Holy Scripture, is St. Paul.[4] We are at present in the midst of a Pauline renaissance. Because of what Paul and his writings have meant in my own life and thought, it is naturally very gratifying to me personally that today his status in the world of critical Biblical scholarship should be so very different from what it was half a century or less ago, when his strong voice first spoke to me. In those days many influential voices proclaimed the great Tarsan to be the perverter of the Christian religion, the man who transformed the simple faith of Jesus into mystical reverie and compli-

---

[4] Among recent studies which uphold the Pauline authorship of this disputed Epistle, the arguments adduced by Ernst Percy in his massive work, *Die Probleme der Kolosser- und Epheserbriefe* (Lund, 1946), will doubtless remain for many years the most comprehensive as well as the most conclusive. It is greatly to be regretted that C. Leslie Mitton (as he acknowledges in his Preface) had no access to Percy's volume while writing his recent book, *The Epistle to the Ephesians, Its Authorship, Origin and Purpose* (Oxford, 1951), in which he finally decides against Paul's authorship of Ephesians.

cated theology. But, in the course of these last decades, partly because New Testament study has acquired again the dimension of depth, and partly because tragic happenings associated with two World Wars have been a luminous commentary on Paul's treatment of human nature and his statement of the basic human problem, Gamaliel's most famous disciple and Christianity's most distinguished apostle stands forth in a new light. It is now recognized that there is no conflict, far less abyss, between the teachings of Jesus and the faith of Paul. It has become plain that, as a matter of fact, Paul was the first man in the early Christian community to understand fully the significance of Jesus Christ. The personal experience and independent spirit of the apostle "born out of due time" made him no mere echo or pale reflection of the Jerusalem community. He it was who understood Jesus best, who served Him most, and the pattern of whose life and spirit more closely approximated the mind of Christ than that of any man who ever lived. For this man had also seen the Lord, and the basic tenets which he proclaimed had come from a personal unveiling of Jesus Christ to him and in him. Paul knew the history of Christ; he prized the tradition about Christ. But he was what he was, and said what he said, because of "the revelation of Jesus Christ." And never, we might add, was the reality of Revelation more obvious and the reflective powers of the Apostle's mind more transfigured, than in the great book which is known by the title, *The Epistle to the Ephesians*.

It is important to observe that this document is a *letter*. It is not an oracle, such as an Old Testament prophet would deliver. It is not an impersonal theological treatise such as many of Paul's successors in Christian reflection have produced. It is a letter which he, as a member of the early Christian community, wrote to fellow members of that community. They and he together belonged to the "Fellowship of the Spirit," that is, to the "Fellowship created by the Spirit." They had passed through the experience of the new life in Christ. Paul was interested in their education.

He wanted to tell them who they really were, what it was that had happened to them, what the implications of their experience and of their communal life were on the road of time and in the endless vista of eternity. Above all, he wished them to know who this Jesus Christ really was in all the majesty of his person and work and cosmic meaning.

Yet, though only a letter, this document was not lacking in authority. Paul, like the other apostolic writers, spoke with all the authority of the Old Testament prophet. His authority derived from his prophetic consciousness, from the awareness that Jesus Christ Himself had called him, and had unfolded to him the "mystery." His momentary status in a Roman prison was that of a "steward," that is, of an "executor" of the "mystery." A secret hitherto hidden in God had been made manifest to him and he was required to unveil it to others. It was Paul who first grasped, in all its grandeur, the significance of the new Christian community, and who proclaimed the cosmic implications of this new unity which had come into being in Christ.

As the "executor" of this "mystery," this unveiled secret, Paul was fully aware of, and duly exercised about, his Apostolic authority. But his "open secret" he made known to his fellow Christians not with imperious, Olympic gestures, nor in the grand manner of Moses whose face so shone in his descent from the "Holy Mount" that the people could not look upon it. The sublimest communication ever made to men was made from a Roman prison by one who in his own esteem was "the very least of all the saints" (3:8) in the Christian community, one who regarded himself "a prisoner of Jesus Christ" for their sake to whom he wrote, that their minds might be illumined by his words, and their hearts receive fresh courage from his "tribulations" for them which were their "glory" (3:13).

But Paul was as priestly in his sympathy as he was prophetic in his utterance. He loved people "with the affection of Jesus Christ," he "travailed in birth" that Christ might be formed in people. When we contemplate the priestly tenderness of St. Paul, which gave fragrance and beauty to the prophetic majesty of his thought, we can understand how it was that Rembrandt, the greatest of painters, steeped himself in Paul's writings in order that he might "interpret the divine Companion in terms of the infinite, all-embracing, tenderness of Christ" (Baldwin Brown).

This Letter is an *ecumenical* letter. It was addressed to no church in particular, but to all the churches and to all Christians in general, wherever these were to be found throughout the whole "oikumene," that is, the "inhabited earth." The earliest manuscripts of the Epistle have no reference to Ephesus, and there is nothing in the text that gives it any local coloring. Paul writes "to the saints who are also faithful in Christ Jesus" (1:1) that they might have an understanding of all that it means to be "in Christ."

In this Epistle, therefore, no specific human problem is dealt with. When he wrote to the Galatians, Paul discussed the deadly concepts and the unworthy tactics of the men who were bent upon Judaizing the Christian religion and reducing the young Christian Church to a sect of Judaism. With burning words and blazing indignation he unmasked those who would pervert the Gospel of Christ. He at the same time set forth in their naked simplicity the inmost nature of the Gospel and the core of the Christian life.

When he wrote his first great letter to the Christians in Corinth, Paul had in mind forms of behavior in the life of the local Christian community by which the Gospel was debased. The sublime passage in which he speaks of the institution of the Lord's Supper is set in the sordid background of shameful festive orgies which in the Church in Corinth sometimes preceded the Supper of the Lord.

But here Paul is not thinking of any particular situation, neither of people who tend to pervert the Christian religion nor of people who debase it. He is concerned rather with the permanent situation, both divine and human. When he writes, therefore, it is about the most ultimate and abiding things, about the deepest and most hidden things, in God's redemptive purpose. He writes about the gracious outworking of that purpose in history and beyond history. He describes the divine order which began to become manifest in concrete form when, through faith in Jesus Christ, the grace of God and the need of man came into transforming contact. The opportune moment had arrived for a great ecumenical epistle. The battle for the catholicity of Christianity had been won against the Judaizers who would have made the Christian community a mere Jewish sect. A Christian Church now existed in Rome. There were even "saints in Caesar's household." Small wonder that "Christ's prisoner," living at the center of a world empire, should develop an imperial mind! Could anything be more natural than that Paul, with his native genius for sweeping surveys, his thought fired by the dramatic circumstances of his life and the uniqueness of his environment, and inspired by a special illumination of the Holy Spirit into God's vast purposes, should make, in Christ's name, the imperial pronouncement which is the subject of this study?

d) A COMPENDIUM OF CHRISTIAN TRUTH

The Ephesian Letter has been designated very appropriately *"the crown and climax of Pauline theology."* It holds the same distinction, one ventures to affirm, in relation to the New Testament as a whole. A statement of Dr. J. Scott Lidgett is worth pondering in this connection. For this scholar the Epistle to the Ephesians is "the consummate and most comprehensive statement which even the New Testament contains of the meaning of the Christian religion, blending as no where else its evangelical, spiritual, moral and universal elements. It is certainly the final statement of Pauline theology." [5] The same writer goes on to add,

---

[5] *God in Christ Jesus: A Study of Paul's Epistle to the Ephesians*, by J. Scott Lidgett, p 2.

"Not merely, however, may this Epistle be taken as the crown and climax of the Pauline theology, but of the New Testament as a whole. It stands in very close relation with certain other of the New Testament writings besides those of St. Paul. If this fact is to be properly appreciated, the Epistle must be set side by side with St. John XIV to XVII, with the First Epistle of St. John and with the First Epistle of St. Peter." [6] We might speak of this Letter, indeed, as the distilled essence of the Christian religion, the most authoritative and most consummate compendium of our holy Christian faith.

A few simple allusions will serve by comparison to illustrate and confirm this judgment.

In the *Epistle to the Galatians* Paul set forth and vindicated the objective and essentially evangelical character of the Christian message to mankind. Salvation was by faith in Jesus Christ without the works of the Law. In the *Epistle to the Romans,* he descanted upon the "Righteousness of God," God's gracious coming into history in Jesus Christ, which, when accepted by Jew or Gentile, relates the soul, in the most intimate and victorious way, to God Himself and to the new order of His righteousness in Christ Jesus. But, in the Ephesian Epistle the truth of the Gospel, which Paul established with cogent arguments in his fiery polemic to the Galatian Christians, is taken for granted as an accepted and blessed reality. The strife of tongues has here ceased, and no note of controversy is echoed by the apostolic pen. Both they that "were far off" and they that "are nigh" were reconciled to God by the Cross. In the Epistle to the Romans, the affirmation regarding the blessedness of those who submit to the Righteousness of God, comes at the close of massive and intricate reasoning; in the great Ecumenical Letter this blessedness is the exultant starting point. The end of dialectic becomes the beginning of rhapsody: "Blessed be the God and Father of our Lord

---

[6] *Id.,* p. 3.

Jesus Christ, who has blessed us in Christ" with every spiritual blessing in the heavenly places. (1:3).

The breadth of Paul's interest and the range of his vision in the Ephesian Letter are both equally amazing. His *interest* embraces all that God has done *for* man, what He has done *in* man and what He does and can do *through* man. To use theological language, the great redemptive facts of the Christian faith are here set forth in their objective splendor. There follows a moving description of Christian experience, that spiritual inwardness which characterizes life when it is renewed by the Holy Spirit and is lived "in Christ." Then comes an affirmation of the essentially active and militant nature of Christian living. The Christian must be truly Christian in every relationship of life. Moreover, in view of subtle and potent adversaries, who constantly beset his path, the permanent pattern of his life in history must be one of vigilant alertness and of soldierly courage. Christian doctrine, Christian experience, and Christian ethics are inseparably related.

No less striking is the *range* of the Apostle's vision. All the aeons from eternity to eternity come within his ken. His gaze moves from "before the foundation of the world" (1:4), to the time beyond time, when time reaches its "fullness," and God "gathers together in one all things in Christ" (1:10). He spans in thought the immensities of space to their uttermost frontiers. The orbit of his soaring imagination is not only "all things in heaven and in earth" (1:10); its extreme poles are "far above all heavens" (4:10) and the "lower regions of the earth" (4:9). The ultimate spiritual unity which he contemplates is so rich that, within its all embracing scope, will be brought together in unison, God and man, man and woman, Jew and Gentile, master and servant. Out of this boundless diversity God shall establish, with Christ as its center, a United Kingdom of Heaven and Earth, a great divine Commonwealth, a majestic scheme of cosmic relations.

e) DOCTRINE SET TO MUSIC

This "vision splendid" Paul presents in form and language consonant with its greatness. He infuses into the glowing product of his imagination the melody of his ecstatic spirit. If ever sweetness was wedded to light in a literary production, it is in the *Epistle to the Ephesians*.

This Letter is pure music. More than one scholar has noted its musical structure and quality. What we read here is truth that sings, doctrine set to music. Some have drawn attention to the liturgical character of the Epistle. Edgar J. Goodspeed speaks about "this great liturgical meditation upon the supreme worth of Christianity." [7] The rhapsodic outburst of thanksgiving with which it begins has been called "one of the first manifestations of the early Christian genius for liturgy," and chapters one and two, a "Jubilate over the blessedness of the Christian Salvation." [8] What is certain is that the sequence of ideas is liturgical rather than coldly logical. The Epistle must be read aloud if the meaning and grandeur of this first liturgy of the Christian Church are to become apparent.

The keynote to this great liturgical composition is the third verse of the first chapter, which begins, "Blessed be the God and Father of our Lord Jesus Christ." Here the "Prisoner of Jesus" lets himself go; he "hurls his heart into a paean." This rhapsodical utterance has been compared to the "overture of an opera, foreshadowing the successive melodies that are to follow."

Paul breaking into ecstasy becomes the very soul of the Christian religion, as the sublimest exponent of the "music of eternity." One cannot but compare and contrast his mood with that of Greek philosopher and Hebrew Rabbi. For the great thinkers of the Golden Age of Athens, as for the German philosopher Hegel, in a later period, it was the crowning glory of philosophic thought

---

[7] *The Meaning of Ephesians*, p. 10.　　　[8] *Id.*, p. 22.

to apply serene reflection to what had already been achieved in reality, in order to discover and interpret its truth. "The owl of Minerva takes her flight when the shades of night have fallen." First, consummation, then thought exercised upon it. For the great Jewish Rabbis, Gamaliel, for example, the supreme truth of love still awaited its unveiling; it would become manifest with the coming of the Messiah. But for Paul the real and the true had come in God's great act in Jesus Christ. Therefore, not like the owl of Minerva who set out in the evening twilight to engage in calm reflection upon an order which had been completed, but, like an eagle, Paul rises in thought, at a time of universal despondency, to greet and announce the birth of a new order which had arrived. It was a time for music and good cheer.

The musical quality of Paul's thought in the Ephesian Letter, as he envisions God's Order, coincides with the essentially musical character of the Bible as a whole. All the great movements in the Biblical drama of creation and redemption have a musical accompaniment. At nature's dawn the "morning stars sang together, and all the sons of God shouted for joy." An orchestra of Angels hailed the Advent of the "Child born, the Son given." At history's close there will be a "Grand Finale." The trumpets shall sound. Dryden, the seventeenth century poet, has caught in magnificent verse what is at the heart of God's great scheme of things.

> From harmony, from heavenly harmony
>   This universal frame began:
>   From harmony to harmony
> Through all the compass of the notes it ran,
> The diapason closing full in Man.
>
> . . . .
>
> As from the power of sacred lays
>   The spheres began to move,
> And sung the great Creator's praise
>   To all the blest above;

> So when the last and dreadful hour
> This crumbling pageant shall devour,
> The trumpet shall be heard on high,
> The dead shall live, the living die,
> And Music shall untune the sky.[9]

What else could the Christian religion be but a singing religion? Its sweetest songs are "Songs in the night"; its most rapturous music had its birth in some prison. For, in confinement,

> Because the heart is saddest
> The lyre's tense strings are gladdest.

In a Toledo dungeon John of the Cross wrote the sublimest of mystic lyrics. The *Pilgrim's Progress,* literature's most famous and most triumphant allegory, was composed by John Bunyan in a Bedford jail. Out of servitude came the "Negro Spirituals," the divinest Christian minstrelsy in the Americas. From a prison cell, in the Rome of the Caesars, came *The Epistle to the Ephesians.*

f) THE MOST CONTEMPORARY BOOK IN THE BIBLE

St. Paul lived in the Post-Augustan age of Roman history. It had been the dream of the great Augustus to give the Roman Empire a perfect and permanent constitution; and he died in the conviction that he had done so. But in Paul's time, not so many decades after Augustus' death, life in Rome, and throughout the Empire, was marked by a process of social disintegration, and by a sense of futility and loss of nerve on the part of individuals. It was in this kind of situation that Paul proclaimed the Order of God.

Today we can look in retrospect at other orders which in their time bore all the marks of permanency and which nevertheless have passed away. We live in the Post-Constantine age, a time in which the imposing unity of Church and State has been shattered,

---

[9] John Dryden, *Song for St. Cecilia's Day.*

bringing to an end, in the most representative areas of the world, the special secular privileges of the Christian religion. We live also in the Post-Victorian age. That is, we live in a period in which the illusion of automatic progress has been shattered, when men no longer believe in inevitable evolutionary advance. Some would say indeed that we lived in the Post-Christian age. This is not true, if it means that Christianity has ceased to grow and to have vitality. It is true, however, in the important sense that we have now entered a period in the history of Western man when Christian axioms and assumptions no longer constitute the basis of his thought or action. Our dominant culture and our prevailing political activity have ceased, to a major extent, to be inspired by Christian principles.

A greatly intensified version of Paul's Post-Augustan era is ours. Nihilism and pessimism are hallmarks of Western Culture in our time. What is Nihilism? The spirit of Nihilism is, as Nietzsche put it, "to have sought a meaning in life that wasn't there." We live in a great void and suffer from universal disillusionment. "All truth alters," multitudes say, "and the lights of earth are out."

Pessimism is the dominant mood. After all, what matters anyhow? What is the use? "Our deeds are hopes split on the glitterless dark." As for civilization, has not a popular philosopher said: "The more civilized we become, the more incapable of maintaining civilization we are."

It is clear that no advance in our knowledge of nature or of our control over it can be of any avail to us. The vastness of our understanding of nature and its forces is, indeed, in the present state of human relations, a very large part of our problem. We know far too much for our welfare; our scientific knowledge is too great for our goodness. If Einstein should be declared correct in the formula he has proposed to unify that sector of the world in which electromagnetic forces are regnant with the world controlled by the force of gravitation, the real problem of our time will not have been touched. All that will have been accomplished will be another decisive contribution to the physical unity of the world in the background of spiritual disunity, with its nihilism and pessimism.

Unity of a quite different kind is needed. Men need to be united in a common outlook upon the meaning of life and in a buoyant approach to the problems of life. This is the kind of unity that opens up before us in Paul's Ephesian Letter. A study of this New Testament writing offers three things which our generation most desperately needs.

1. *This Letter proclaims the essential image.* Amid the Nihilism of our time, when men are desperately trying to make sure of their existence, searching earnestly for some usable mythology, and pledging their loyalty to some daring and meaningful symbol, yesterday to Fasces and Swastika, today to the Hammer and Sickle, Paul proclaims the essential image. That image is the figure of Jesus Christ. Christ is the token that God wills fellowship, that love is the ultimate reality. Christ is the center of a community, the Church, which is designed by God to be the precursor of a vast cosmic society. This is the image which a poet of our time, in the spirit of St. Paul, puts into the mouth of the wise men of the East, the representatives of human wisdom, upon their arrival at a Bethlehem stable: "Oh, here and now our endless journey stops." [10] Christ is the essential image. To "know" Him, to explore what He means for God and man, for history terrestrial and history celestial, is to obtain the clue to life's meaning and discover the core of life's reality. Then like shadows at daybreak, the myths and symbols, which have provided earnest men with light to interpret the world and with strength to live in it, pass away. Then we come to learn afresh that fellowship and not a "barbed-wire existence" is what God has designed for his children. We awaken to the fact that brotherhood has cultural significance, and that human knowledge with-

---

[10] W. H. Auden in *A Christmas Oratorio.*

out human brotherhood is vanity. And surveying the embattled frontiers of the earth and sensing their intolerable tensions, we proclaim the truth that forgiveness and mercy have political power.

2. The Ephesian Letter *presents the basic structure* which humanity needs for the true expression of communal life. That structure is the fellowship of believers in Jesus Christ, which constitutes the essence of what we call the Christian Church. The Church is the universal community designed by God to transcend and embrace all differences of race, station and sex that divide mankind. It constitutes the pattern for all true community, so that the surest way to achieve human harmony in the secular order is to extend the bounds of the Christian community throughout the world. For it is in the measure in which men are reconciled to God, practice the worship of God, seek the Kingdom of God, and live with one another in peace as Christian brethren, that society shall be influenced, directly and indirectly, to seek peace and concord.

The fact, moreover, cannot be too greatly stressed that it is only in the fellowship of the Church, through worship and discipline, through the assumption of responsibility, according to one's talents and opportunities, and loyal cooperation in common tasks, that men and women are fitted for the life of citizenship in society. As members of the Christian fellowship men come to learn that lesson upon which the very possibility of creative human living is based, namely, that life is not a treadmill but a school. It is surely significant that in the glowing thought of St. Paul the life and history of the Christian Church constitutes the chief lesson book in which spirits higher than human spirits, the Principalities and Powers in the heavenly sphere, will receive their deepest lesson into the "manifold [the many-colored] wisdom of God." Not only so, but it is only in the Christian community, when its corporate life functions as it ought, that men in general can be taught, by concrete illustration, the meaning of that abundant, exuberant, sacrificial self-giving which alone constitutes true life. Only in the Church when it is truly the Church do men find an institution where goodness overflows like a fountain and is not merely contained as in a cistern. Life's cisterns are empty, its wells are exhausted, because men fail to relate themselves to that community whose needs are supplied from the Fountain of Life.

3. The Ephesian Letter is supremely relevant to our situation today because it *provides truth with a lilt*.

Truth is needed not only as an image and as a system, but also and above all as a melody. We dare not fail to recognize, of course, that our chaotic time needs ordered truth, a structure of truth. The generation before ours, because it lived in halcyon, romantic days, disliked doctrine and developed an anti-dogmatic complex. Disillusionment and the sensed need of an intelligible world view have shaken our generation out of its anti-dogmatic slumbers. To order our lives and wend our pilgrim way amid the perplexities of this present time we need a system of thought, and a massive luminous system at that. In a world where Marxism and other thought systems hostile to Christianity make constant progress we can understand and appreciate what William Blake meant when he said, "I must create a system or be enslaved by another man's."

But it is even more important that thought should have a lilt than that it should have a system. The truth we need is truth that sings. And the singing must have the note of hope and victory in it. For of the music of disorder and despair we have had enough. Our generation has listened to this music. We have heard the vaunt: "My music is an iron starry shout." We have been regaled with the glorification of uncertainty. "My suns are born to briefness like a spark." What we need is the music of faith.

This music the Marxists have. A cold proposition, however true it may be regarded to be, has no dynamic power. To say that matter is what is ultimate does not stir anybody. But to affirm that materialism has the key and promise of the future can start a crusade. For this is something to get excited about; here is a cause to get into. The old materialism was academic; the new dialectical materialism of Marx and Lenin is dynamic. Believing that the radiant invincible forces of the universe are on its side it creates song:

> Arise ye prisoners of starvation!
> Arise ye wretched of the earth!
> For justice thunders condemnation;
> A better world's in birth.

The first thing the Chinese Communists did on arriving in a new community on their southward march in China was to teach the people to sing; and after that to dance.

No doctrine, however true, that does not have a lilt to it can meet modern Marxism with its crusading passion. But Christianity, which is itself the "music of eternity," has not only given birth to great music, to the Chorals of Bach and the *Messiah* of Handel, to Luther's Cradle Song and the Negro Spirituals; it has also given birth to thoughts that sing. Such are the thoughts of Paul in the Ephesian Letter.

We now turn, therefore, to study in a more intimate way that doctrinal foundation of orchestral melody, which is Paul's Epistle to the Ephesians.

CHAPTER II

The Great Rift

The universe is rifted. History and the heart of man are rifted. The fact of a rift is the elemental, decisive fact about reality in its wholeness.

In the background of the vast scheme of reconciliation which forms the central theme of the Epistle to the Ephesians, and which we have called God's Order, there exists a condition of total spiritual disorder. This disorder not only characterizes the inner life of man and his relations with his fellows; it involves a state of conflict in man's relationship to God, and even of internecine strife "in the heavenly places," that is, within the supernatural sphere itself. Throughout the entire universe disharmony reigns; the cosmos is split. In the supramundane realm are "principalities," "powers," "world rulers of this present darkness," "spiritual hosts of wickedness in the heavenly places" (6:12), who oppose the will of God, the Creator; while on earth a fierce "enmity" (2:16) is rampant, separating men from God and from fellowmen. Sin looms everywhere as a cosmic fact. The universe is the scene of a widespread revolt against the authority of God. The lordship of the Almighty is disputed, and a spiritual conflict rages.

It is important to observe that the universal dualism here alluded to is not an absolute or an ultimate dualism. It is, however, a *real* dualism. It is not a duality constituted by a mere difference of viewpoint, such as the classical distinction between sense and reason. It is more than a dualism in appearance, a mere mental interpretation of diverse or contradictory phenomena. There is in the universe a very real and grave conflict of spiritual forces; but it is not absolute: it is not inherent in the constitution of the universe. There are not two original principles or powers. The Universe has its being in one God, who is "Father of all," "above all, through all, and in all" (4:6), of whom "every family in heaven and on earth is named" (3:15), and who "created all things" (3:9). While it is true that the supremacy of God in the Universe is being disputed in a real manner by supernatural forces, and while the life of those human beings who seek to obey God is one of conflict "in the middle and heart of the universal battle," victory will belong to God, who will establish his spiritual order in Christ (1:21), in whom the lost unity of creation will be restored. For God is the King of Eternity; while the aberrant forces that oppose him are finite and belong only to time. There is no suggestion in Paul's world-view of a finite Deity who is confronted by inexorable cosmic forces which, in their native right and their uncreated might, challenge his lordship.

a) THE TRANSCENDENTAL RIFT

There was no systematic Christian view of the universe in the first Century, and we should not look for a fully elaborated world-view in St. Paul. Yet certain things are clear. According to the Ephesian Letter, there exist two distinct realms, a transcendental or supramundane realm, and a terrestrial realm. Paul speaks of the first as the "heavenly sphere," "the heavenly places"

(1:3), which have a beyondness which he describes as "above all heavens"; the second is the "earth" (1:10), beneath which are the "lower parts of the earth" (4:9). The temporal form and span of the terrestrial is "this age" (1:21). The Rift is not the fact that two such diverse realms exist. The Rift passes through both realms, and cleaves each assunder.[1]

The rift "in the heavenly places" is of decisive importance because it projects itself into the mundane, historical sphere of human life. The "heavenly sphere" in the Epistle to the Ephesians is not what is ordinarily meant by Heaven as a future state of perfect bliss. It differs also from the Johannine sphere of Life and Truth. For included in it are not only aspects of blessedness but also supernatural forces of evil. "Hosts of wickedness" live and act in the "heavenlies." On the other hand, Christ is enthroned in this sphere, and people who are "in Christ" dwell within it. But while those who are "in Christ" belong there, and the true source and center of their life is there, the "heavenly sphere" is no less the abode of the tremendous "spiritual hosts of wickedness" (6:12) to combat whom the Christian needs the "whole armor of God" (6:13).

So important for our understanding of Paul's thought is this concept of the "heavenly sphere," that I quote here an admirable statement regarding it by J. Armitage Robinson, whose book, *St. Paul's Epistle to the Ephesians,* is probably the finest and most complete study extant on the great Pauline Letter. "The heavenly sphere," says Dr. Robinson, "is the sphere of spiritual activities: that immaterial region, the 'unseen universe,' which lies behind the world of sense. In it great forces are at work: forces which are conceived of as having an order and constitution of their own; as having in part transgressed against that order, and so having become disordered: forces which in part are opposed to us and wrestle against us: forces again which take an intelligent interest

---

[1] For an interesting study of Paul's world-view, see Hugo Odeberg, *The View of the Universe in the Epistle to the Ephesians* (Lunds Universitets Årsskrift N.F., I, 29).

in the purpose of God with this world, and for which the story of man is an object-lesson in the many-sided wisdom of God: forces, over all of which, be they evil or be they good, Christ is enthroned, and we in Him." [2]

A Master Strategist of Evil

One of the "rulers of this present darkness" Paul personalizes and names. He calls him the "Prince of the power of the air, the spirit that is now at work in the sons of disobedience" (2:2), and also, simply, the "Devil," against whose "wiles" Christians are enjoined to be on their guard (6:11).

In taking seriously a personal, supernatural spirit of evil in the Universe, Paul does no more than follow Biblical thought as a whole. For the Bible, let it be pointed out, speaks less of evil in general and more of the Evil One. The fact cannot be escaped that for Jesus a personal Devil was a tremendous reality. He was much more than a mythological representation of a sinister squint in human nature or an evil trend in history. And who will dare affirm that Jesus, with His exquisite sensitivity to God and His personal knowledge of God, should not be taken seriously when he alleges the real existence of a supernatural spirit who challenges the hierarchical principle that the will of the Creator must be supreme over all grades of being, and who himself incarnates the breach of this principle? It need not surprise us, therefore, that Paul of Tarsus, who possessed to an unparalleled degree the mind of Christ, should have the same view as his Master with respect to the nature and dimension of the spiritual struggle which human beings are doomed to wage in history.

After a long period during which, under the influence of Rationalism and the projection of an evolutionary hypothesis into human and cosmic history, the figure of the Devil was simply a mythological attempt to explain the existence of evil in the world, the intellectual climate surrounding this whole problem

---
[2] J. Armitage Robinson, *St. Paul's Epistle to the Ephesians*, p. 21.

begins to change. The sordid and disillusioning happenings of the past generation have raised afresh in many earnest minds the hypothesis of a strategy of evil carried out by a spiritual power who is ill-disposed towards human welfare. It is, at the same time, being recognized that, philosophically speaking, no well-grounded rational or metaphysical reason can be adduced as to why in the cosmic hierarchy there should not be spirits other or higher than human spirits; why some of these spirits should not have made Evil their Good; and why their activities should not be coordinated by a master strategist.

Whatever views a person may hold on this subject, he may as well face the fact that the question of his Satanic Majesty, the Devil, has been reopened in the thought of our time. Foremost among those who have brought back the Devil as a topic for intellectual discussion are two laymen. One of these is the Oxford teacher of English literature, C. S. Lewis; the other is Denis de Rougemont, a young French Swiss author. Lewis' now famous *Screwtape Letters* resuscitates the figure of Satan as a contemporary force. In terms of the traditional "Arch-fiend," transformed in the mid-twentieth Century into a polished and up-to-date mentor of modern men and women, Lewis traces the pattern and points to the source of much popular philosophy in the life of today. This he does in a vein of gay and biting sarcasm, which is entirely in keeping with traditional opinion regarding the sensitivities of the Great Deceiver, and is in harmony with the sound psychological principle that no one so dislikes being made fun of as one who is radically insincere. So Lewis laughs at the Devil.

De Rougemont in his book, *The Devil's Share*, has much to say that is both popular and profound on the same subject. He makes a particularly telling reference to the French poet Baudelaire and to his view on the Satan question. "In Baudelaire's *Short Prose Poems*," says de Rougemont, "we find the most profound observation on Satan written by a modern: 'The Devil's cleverest wile is to convince us that he does not exist. God says, 'I am He who is.' But the Devil, ever jealous of God and bent on imitating Him, even though it be in reverse (since he sees everything from below) says to us, like Ulysses to the Cyclops, 'My name is *Nobody*. There is Nobody, whom should you be afraid of? Are you going to tremble before the non-existent?' " [3]

Nothing is so indicative, however, of a soberer and more realistic intellectual outlook upon the shadow side of existence as the renaissance of John Milton which is taking place in contemporary literature. After a long period of eclipse, Milton and his great epic, *Paradise Lost,* are returning to favor. Milton is coming back because our generation, aware that it is "lost," looks for clues as to the origin and meaning of its lostness. Milton's presentation of a hierarchical universe in which spiritual unity and moral integrity depend upon obedience to the will of God, and in which finite spirits became "lost" because of their pride and disobedience, offers much food for serious reflection. Central in the epic are the figures of the "Lost Arch-angel" and of man whom he seduced. Literally nothing in secular literature is more germane to the spiritual problem of our time than a study of Milton's Satan.

In the quaint language of Jacob Boehme, quoted by Denis de Rougemont, Satan fell because he "wanted to become an author." That is, he wanted to originate something of his own, of which he would be the creator and sustainer. In the impressive mythology of *Paradise Lost* the head of Satan gave birth to Sin, the principle of disobedience. In the dread entrails of Sin, Satan's daughter, the foul monster Death, was engendered, by the amorous action of the father himself. These two, Sin and Death stand guard at Hell's portals.

How did the celestial seraph become the Prince of Hell? Through "pride and worse ambition." He would "seek himself a glory above his peers." "He trusted to have equaled the Most High." Here is his own account:

---

[3] *The Devil's Share,* p. 17.

> Lifted up so high,
> I disdained subjection, and thought one step higher
> Would set me highest, and in a moment quit
> The debt immense of endless gratitude,
> So burdensome, still paying, still to owe:
> Forgetful what from Him I still received;
> And understood not that a grateful mind
> By owing owes not, but still pays, at once
> Indebted and discharged — What burden then?

Satan was irked by being a creature and by having to show gratitude for gifts received. He wanted to be God, to be a Creator in his own right, and so to owe nothing to any higher. He therefore rebelled and fought, and lost. Frustrated, he transvalued all values. "Evil be thou my Good; by thee at least divided empire with Heaven's King I hold." He was unhappy, and experienced twinges of remorse, yet would he not repent but exulted in the proud misery which he called freedom:

> To reign is worth ambition, though in Hell;
> Better to reign in Hell than serve in Heaven.

Little by little the "lost Archangel" lost every trace of spiritual nobility. He who aspired to be God became literally the Devil, though the manifestation of traits which, because of their unutterable meanness, men are accustomed to call "devilish." Satan assaulted man out of pure jealousy. In the satanic evolution which followed, we can detect the equivalent of a second "Fall." In a little book entitled, *A Preface to Paradise Lost*, C. S. Lewis, himself a modern disciple of John Milton, has thus summarized what might be described as the progressive satanization of the Devil, which process the reader of the sublime epic can follow and verify for himself by perusing its several books. Says the Oxford professor: "From hero to general, from general to politician, from politician to secret service agent, and thence to a thing that peers in at bedroom or bathroom windows, and thence to a toad, and finally to a snake—such is the progress of Satan." [4] Lewis goes on to discuss the view commonly held that Milton, realizing that he had begun by making Satan too glorious, introduces the subsequent marks of degeneration in order to "rectify the error." But he rightly rejects this interpretation and adds: "We need not doubt that it was the poet's intention to be fair to evil, to give it a run for its money—to show it first at the height, with all its rants and melodrama and 'Godlike imitated state' about it, and *then* to trace what actually becomes of such self-intoxication when it encounters reality."

Not only does the moral character of the Devil become increasingly base and banal, but his insight, both intellectual and spiritual, suffers eclipse. He becomes blind to reality. Milton would seem to be committed to the proposition that "the Devil is (in the long run) an ass." There is in him intellectual brilliance, but with a total incapacity to understand anything. "This doom," comments Lewis, "he has brought upon himself; in order to avoid seeing one thing, he has, almost voluntarily, incapacitated himself from seeing all. And thus, throughout the poem, all his torments come, in a sense, at his own bidding, and the Divine judgment might have been expressed in the words '*thy* will be done.' He says, 'Evil be thou my Good' (which includes Nonsense be thou my Sense), and his prayer is granted." [5] We might be reading the character and life history of contemporary tyrants who, wanting to remake the world in their own image and direct it according to their own will, become impersonal forces to which man is subject.

"*Principalities and Powers*"

A very real aspect of the Rift which cleaves the Universe is the presence of inexorable Forces or Powers of an impersonal character which affect terrestrial life and frustrate human aspiration. Even should the view be taken, which I believe to be philo-

---

[4] *A Preface to Paradise Lost*, C. S. Lewis, p. 97.   [5] *Id.*, p. 96.

sophically unwarrantable, Biblically unsound, and religiously perilous, that there is in the Universe no personal power of evil, there still remain "things in heaven": Principalities and Powers. These forces, however they be interpreted in their ultimate nature, are realities to be reckoned with in history, because human history is in many crucial respects controlled by them. Whether mythological or not, these Forces are devastatingly real. They exercise potent sway over mankind. Time and again they blast human hopes and conduce to the "Vanity of Human Wishes."

From one point of view, such Powers may be regarded as judicial processes which go into action whenever the principle of obedience to God is violated by finite spirits. In this respect they are laws of the moral order, or we might say, of a violated moral order. When finite spirits, whose true being and destiny consists in loyal obedience to infinite goodness, transgress the constituted order, the direst consequences follow. The Greeks spoke about "Nemesis" and the "Furies" which trailed the steps of transgressors. The Hebrews proclaimed that the "Stars in their courses fought against Sisera," that is, against every violator of elemental righteousness. St. Paul in the first Chapter of his Epistle to the Romans paints a lurid but perfectly realistic picture of the consequences that result, the judgment and the wrath, when the principles of moral virtue are disobeyed. We have come to see that "world history is world judgment." We are forced to recognize in history a dialectic, a "process whereby history defeats itself." When any human good is clutched and cherished and made the Sovereign Good, it produces its opposite. When science is hailed as the world Savior, it produces a weapon which creates world gloom and foreshadows world destruction. When civilization is pursued as an end in itself, a psychology is produced in the "civilized," which makes it difficult for civilization to maintain itself. The poetic insight of Francis Thompson is literally true on the plane of world history.

> All things forsake thee, who forsakest me.

The "Era of Monsters," which is still dragging out its course, has led many sober minds in our generation to recognize in the Pauline "Principalities and Powers," the deified expression of finite realities, which, when absolutized, that is, elevated to the status of the Divine, exercise a sinister and uncontrollable influence upon human affairs. The moment some race, nation or class, exalts itself above "everything called God and that is worshipped," aberrant religions of a secular character make their appearance. In these last times we have witnessed history in reverse. The ancient pagan deities, whose exit from their traditional shrines upon the advent of Christ Milton with poetic license describes in a famous poem, become enshrined again in political systems. To the spiritual renaissance of this "damned crew," as Milton calls them in his Nativity Ode, are traceable a multitude of our present woes.

But quite apart from the reality of a judicial process in history, and the baneful might of secular divinities, the historical life of mankind is controlled, and frequently enserfed, by other "Powers" of a transcendental order, which take the form of thought systems. Ideas of whatever kind, be they true or false, exercise a most potent sovereignty in human affairs. What has Rationalism, for example not done to enchain the human mind, making it impossible to see and unpopular to allege to see, anything beyond the very circumscribed confines of its myopic dogmatism? Ideological tyranny is one of the most universal and sinister forms of tyranny. The most acute phase of the present crisis in world history derives from the transcendental power of dialectical Materialism. In Christian circles a similar Power has wrought untold harm. The application of principles of pure rationalism to the study of the Bible, whereby ideas regarded as self-evident are used in Biblical interpretation, both by the theologically heterodox and the theologically orthodox alike, constitutes one of the "Principalities and Powers in high places" which destroy the insight and weaken the witness of many followers of Jesus Christ.

b) THE HISTORICAL RIFT

In dealing in the preceding section with the Transcendental Rift, we have considered the question of a supramundane order which is the seat of forces, personal or impersonal, which exert a controlling influence upon human life. We turn now to consider man himself, and the rift which exists in human nature, together with the doleful consequences of this rift in the life of mankind. We will begin with the Biblical interpretation of man, very especially with the view of man's actual estate as set forth by St. Paul in the Epistle to the Ephesians.

Man in Biblical Thought

Man as we know him, the being variously described as "natural," "common" "average" man, is in the thought of St. Paul, man "without God," and so "without hope in the world" (2:12). Because God does not occupy the central place in his allegiance and does not operate as the central force in his life, man in his historical existence is in a hopeless, a desperate plight. He is "dead," immersed, buried, in "trespasses and sins" (2:1); that is to say, he lives doing wrong and missing the mark. He follows the "Prince of the Power of the Air, the spirit that is now at work in the sons of disobedience" (2:2), which means that not God but a rebel power is man's Master. His life is marked by the predominance of fleshly lusts and he is the slave of carnal appetites and mental whims. All men are thus "children of wrath" (2:3); they pass their lives at variance with life's true course, and in consequence suffer the consequences of their misguided ways. Attempts on men's part to right their situation are useless, for they "live in the vanity [or futility] of their minds" (4:17). They suffer from spiritual blindness, being "darkened in their understanding" (4:18). They lack true light because they live apart from the true life, "alienated from the life of God." And they live thus on account of "their hardness of heart," because they are inured in their ways, unwilling to reverse themselves and give serious consideration to any other point of view or way of living. But commitment to a purely humanistic, secularistic existence makes them "callous"; their moral fibre decays and they degenerate into "licentiousness," ever conjuring up for their indulgence new ways of immoral behavior (4:19).

In such terms Paul describes man and the human problem, and brings home to the far-flung readers of his ecumenical letter that these traits summed up the "old nature" (4:22) in which men in general lived. This was the nature which they as Christians were called to "put off" through becoming "renewed in the spirit of their minds" (4:23) by acquiring, that is to say, a total change of outlook. The "new nature," which is to be substituted for the old, is "created after the likeness of God in true righteousness and holiness" (4:24); it is a Godlike nature which expresses itself in conformity to the will of God, which is "righteousness," and in consecration to the reality of God which is "holiness."

Keeping in mind this description of man as he is, which Paul gives us in the maturest of his writings, let us consider its meaning and implications. Let us, that is to say, interpret man, in the dual light of Biblical thought and historical life.

What is man? That is the decisive question. Every particular civilization, every specific culture, as well as every system of thought are ultimately based upon a given view of man. So far as history is concerned, as Toynbee has pointed out, man as we know him, so-called "average man," has not appreciably changed in his essential nature in historical time. He is today more or less what he always has been. He seems, moreover, to have learned nothing from experience that is of absolutely decisive importance for his spiritual orientation. "The only thing we learn from history," it has been said, "is that man has never learned anything from history."

In the spirit and language of the Bible man is a being who was made in the image, or likeness of God. He was made *in* love by a God who is love; he was made *for* love, to love God and his fellowmen. God the Creator intended man to be godlike. The only way in which a creature can be *like* his Creator, is in his creatureliness he shall obey the commandment to love. A finite, created being obeys this commandment when he loves God with the love of adoring reverence and loving obedience, and loves his fellow human creatures as himself. But man as we know him in history has aspired to be godlike without God. He has wanted to be like God, in the sense of possessing divine status and divine attributes, without acknowledging God as God. He has had the ambition to be a "God"; hence the significance of the temptation in Genesis (3:5) "Ye shall be as gods." Man has deliriously sought to be like God as God's rival. He has not wanted to be godlike by manifesting as God's child and servant that lowliness and condescension which mark the life of Deity.

And so we have "fallen man," man the sinner, man who has "missed the mark" of achieving true existence, who is "out of step" with reality, who is "off-course" as he seeks his destiny. As we look at rifted human nature, which was split by pride and conditioned towards disobedience, several things need to be stressed. Sin does not have its seat in the lower centers of personality but in the higher. While it leads to the grossest forms of sensuality as the human spirit strays farther and farther "off-course," sin neither had its origin in sensual desire nor does its most awesome expression become manifest in anything pertaining to the body. Sin is a perversity of the mind rather than a debility of the flesh. It has, moreover, a positive as well as a negative manifestation. Negatively it is, in the words of the *Westminster Shorter Catechism*, "any want of conformity unto, or transgression of, the law of God." As such it is a revolt against authority, rebellion against the hierarchical structure of the Universe, the affirmation of self will. But on the positive side, sin is, as already suggested, the pursuit of a false godlikeness. It is the attempt to reach divinity by a short road, to possess God's shining attributes and prerogatives without sharing God's gracious condescension.

There is, undoubtedly, in human nature, as its deepest desire, a yearning for the Infinite and Eternal. God made man like Himself and for Himself, putting Eternity in his heart. Therefore, as Augustine put it "our hearts are restless till they rest in Thee." A contemporary philosopher truly interprets the basic human urge when he says, "Man's whole life is a struggle to gain true existence, an effort to achieve substantiality, so that he may not have lived in vain and vanished like a shadow." [6] But the trouble is that man the sinner has not been satisfied to find his true existence in God and through God. He has wanted rather to have in his own right and as his own possession those things which he regarded as belonging to godlikeness. Since he fell from Being, he has been more interested in *having* than in *being*. He has forgotten that unless he has God he has nothing. Therein lies man's sin and the human problem.

No one knew man and human nature better than Jesus did. On one occasion He put a question to His contemporaries which is the deepest question that was ever asked about man and the most relevant question that can be addressed to our generation. "What shall it profit a man," He asked, "though he should gain the whole world, and lose his own soul [or his own life]" (Matt. 16:26)? Jesus knew, as Paul knew, that man's central drive is a passion to gain, to have, to possess a world, some world, the whole world. The Devil had once made a proposition to Jesus. The proposition was this: He, the "Prince of this world," would give Jesus the whole world as a gift, provided He was prepared to deny God, to be and act "without God," and, worshipping the Devil, join the great Revolt. But for Jesus what really mattered was to be and not to have. For Him true being consisted in a

---

[6] Erich Frank, *Philosophical Knowledge and Religious Understanding*, p. 116.

life lived with God, through God and for God; to such a life things and a world would be added in due course.

On the other hand, the attempt to gain the world leads to the loss of the only world that really matters, the world of the soul, a man's inner life. The pursuit of things, man's acquisitive passion to have, destroys the soul, disintegrates life, makes the human spirit an empty sepulchre, a sepulchre of dead values and blasted hopes.

Apart, however, from the significance of this question which Jesus put to the people of his generation, the Bible abounds both in the Old Testament and in the New with descriptions of divine judgment which bear witness to the tragic consequences for man and human society of the pursuit of false godlikeness. What lurid and dramatic pictures are drawn in the Bible of the total spiritual disintegration which results when man takes his life into his own hands and sets out to forge his own destiny! Demoralization ensues; man becomes dehumanized; his God-given nature upon which God imprinted His own image is defiled. Cain becomes the brazen murderer of his brother. The natural properties of sexual relationship disappear and we have Sodom, with all that "Sodom" means in Biblical history and has come to mean in secular law courts. The perversion of the religious instinct in idol worship becomes, as in the Canaanitish cults, the foul source of indescribable depravity. Paul in his great Epistle to the Romans gives a classical appraisal of the fateful moral aftermath that succeeds the determination to repudiate God, all of which was in the background of his mind when he wrote the Ephesian Letter. Men who "knew God did not honor him as God or give thanks to Him became futile in their thinking and their senseless minds were darkened" (Rom. 1:21). "Because they exchanged the truth about God for a lie and worshiped and served the creature rather than the Creator" (v. 25); "since they did not see fit to acknowledge God, God gave them up to a base mind and to improper conduct" (v. 28).

Not only so: man's Revolt showed itself in confused and embittered social relationships. The great attempt to erect a tower to the glory of man, which would be a perpetual monument to man's divinity and an abiding center of human unity, ended in a linguistic babel and a racial dispersion. For in mankind itself, cut off from God, there is no medium of understanding, nor bond of cohesion. Therefore, what the nation needs, amid the confusion created by a breakdown in an understanding is, in the symbolism of a great Hebrew prophet, a "pure language" which God can give to the peoples of the world. What the peoples of the world require in their isolation and mutual antagonism is a rallying center of unity. This, in the glowing imagery of the Bible, God provides, as we shall see presently, in Jerusalem, the City of God, which, in the unfolding of His purposes, shall succeed the City of Man.

But before the historical consequences of the basic spiritual Rift can be overcome another rift in history of a quite unique character must be overcome also. Paul refers to it in the second chapter of the Ephesian Letter. It is the deep rift between Jew and Gentile. Looked at from the perspective of secular history, this rift has been one of the most bitter and appalling rifts in history. It is the rift, as Paul describes it, between people called Jews who were descended from a common ancestor Abraham, and upon whom the rite of circumcision had been performed, and all non-Jews, bearing the common name of Gentiles, the "nations" who were uncircumcised (Eph. 2). The Gentiles were, in Paul's language, "alienated from the commonwealth of Israel, and strangers to the covenants of promise" (2:12). This rift might appropriately be called the *Sacred Rift*. It was a rift constituted by God Himself between sectors of the human family, which, through the opportunity it offered to deal specifically and redemptively with one sector, would lead, when it was divinely healed, to the eventual healing of the great Rift itself.

Man in Historical Life

What Paul described as the life of sin, the life "without God," what Jesus said happens when men set out to *have* instead of to *be,* has become manifest in our time with particularly impressive and tragic features. Our epoch is a world-wide, ecumenical commentary upon the words of St. Paul, "The wages of sin is death." This is a "Day of the Lord," in which inexorable judicial processes are in operation in human history. Like Jeremiah's contemporaries, but on a vaster scale and in a more tragic context, we and our contemporaries "followed the Bubble and Bubbles became" (G. A. Smith's translation), we "went after empty idols and became empty ourselves" (Moffatt's translation).[7]

A great vacuum, an eerie emptiness, an abysmal void marks human life in our time. We sought in life a meaning that was not there. In consequence, a nihilistic mood pervades every continent. The spectre of Nothingness haunts the world. Even over the United States, a victor nation, there broods a certain Nihilism. The following words were not written of Germany or Japan, or of lands in the Orient or Occident that lie sunk in gloom. They were recently addressed to the American nation by one of her own poets.

> O my country,
> It is Nothing that we must fear: the thought of Nothing:
> The sound of Nothing in our hearts
>   like the hideous scream
> Of fire-engines in the streets at midnight:
> The belief in Nothing.[8]

Two characteristics in particular mark this great vacuum, this loss of a spiritual dimension in our time. One of these is Anonymity, the other is Banality.

When men live "without God" there comes a moment when

---

[7] Jer. 2·5.   [8] "My Country," Davenport.

they begin to live without themselves. They become strange to themselves; they do not know who they are. They are transformed into mere atoms that drift around. They love crowds in which they may lose themselves. They invent all manner of devices to induce self-forgetfulness. Because solitude and silence raise questions as to who they are and where they are going, they hate both. Because music speaks of order and meaning they flee from it. What does anything matter anyhow? Hence the "universal flight into anonymity and enormous cacophony, dominated by the sound of bombs."

When men lose depth and purpose; when far horizons and noble ideals no longer inspire; when "All's one in the end, Republic, Dictator," a certain *banality* invades life. Morbidity and a low grovelling instinct, with a hankering love of novelty and strangeness, make their appearance. People want to be "distracted from distraction by distraction." For that reason what is now designated as "modern" art has become "a museum of social and cultural pathology." No more the shout "Excelsior!"

> Feed our bodies, not our souls
> Fatter body, faster rolls.

Noble ideals are flouted; sordid corruption appears in high places and in low.

But because man was made for something different from this, human nature cannot endure indefinitely a void of this kind with its accompanying anonymity, banality and corruption. Such a situation is always propitious for the outbreak of a war, because in war people become something; they are told what to do, and they lose themselves in something greater than themselves. It is equally favorable for man's submission to superstition, tyranny, and false authority. For when man becomes thoroughly emptied of his humanity, he again raises the question of divinity. Once again it is a choice between God and the "gods," between the fellowship of the saints and the ranks of the "damned crew."

This is the perennial human cycle: Man the sinner, in revolt against God, and refusing to find his true existence in God and his purposes, assumes the lordship of his own life. He strives to acquire great possessions in order to make himself godlike. But his delirious dedication to *having* ends in a loss of *being*, in an empty, disintegrated life, and a purposeless, disordered society. The great Rift, sinnerhood in the "heavenly sphere" and on the plane of human history, creates two supreme problems: the problem of true being for man and the problem of true unity among men. Before we pass on to consider how both these problems are solved by God in the life and relationship of God's Order, let us consider, in brief and summary fashion, some characteristic human attempts, both ancient and modern, to deal with the problem of the great Rift and its consequences.

c) HUMAN APPROACHES TO THE RIFT

Man is so constituted that unity is an indispensable necessity of his nature. He needs unity in the form of an idea to understand life; he needs unity in the form of power in order to control life. The fact of mystery and paradox in the world, the presence of disorder and conflicting forces, makes all the more imperious the demand for unity both by the man of thought and the man of action, by the bad man as well as by the good. Even a system of false thought requires a unity, a logical coherence founded upon a lie or an error; even a Kingdom of Evil demands unity in the form of a common strategy in opposition to Good.

In the course of human history diverse attempts have been made to reduce to a single thought the diversity and disorder by which all things are marked, and to overcome conflict and division by a single policy.

Two paths have been followed to achieve unity: One has been the way of wisdom, and the other the way of power.

The Way of Wisdom

The ancient Greeks, who were the first people to exercise reflective curiosity about the world in which they lived, appeared to be totally unaware of a spiritual rift in the cosmos and in the life of man. Original sin, a native trend towards evil in the human spirit, was quite unreal to them. The Ionians were concerned about discovering the single substance, earth or air, fire or water, to which all nature might be reduced. The Pythagoreans sought in numbers the principle of harmony between the diverse phenomena of Nature. The Stoics found in the universe an immanent logos, an impersonal, unifying principle of order. Plato was aware that the common man was immersed in a life of appetite and sense and was consequently unable to know the Truth or to see the Good. But there was no ultimate rift. By a process of education, which included self-discipline, it was possible, in Plato's view, for the soul to turn towards the Light and to obtain the vision of the Good. At bottom the problem was mental rather than spiritual: How could man achieve true unity of thought, how could he discover the true object of adoration? The solution, the prelude to salvation, was a natural ascent into contemplation and not a supernatural deliverance from bondage.

In modern times the entire problem of unity, whether to understand the world or to harmonize and control it, has been approached from the side of science, and most recently, from the side of technology. The last great world-view which dominated western culture was the attempt to understand the Universe in terms of a cosmic principle of evolution. Since that view broke down, shattered by disillusioning events, no other cosmic philosophy has arisen in representative bourgeois circles. In the democratic world of today there does not exist a great idea, rational or religious, to which common loyalty is given, and which by its luminous character opens up the meaning of life and provides strength to tread the paths of life. Apart from critical histories of philosophy and suggestive philosophies of history, the only thing left in democratic culture which has the semblance of a world-view is a philosophy of freedom. But this philosophy of freedom, this forlorn vestige of intellectual grandeur, is nothing more, at bottom, than a negative freedom, the proclamation of political freedom with no implication of moral responsibility. What is proclaimed is freedom *from* something, not freedom *for* something or *in* something; it is not that freedom which alone is true freedom: captivity to the Eternal.

The abandonment in democratic circles of the attempt to evolve an all embracing world-view has left to science the problem of understanding the world and of determining what man dare hope for. This has tended to make the ideal of knowledge positivistic, the scope of knowledge fragmentary, and the goal of knowledge utilitarian. A scientific culture does not teach man what he *should* do; it does not help him to obtain a vision of life as a whole. It tells him how he can *have* an increasing number of things, while his real problem is a deepening sense of need to *be* something. The facts of the futility of specialization and of technological experts, so far as the knowledge and solution of the ultimate human problem are concerned, have become so familiar by much reiteration, that nothing further needs to be said about them. Only this. It might be well for the cultural positivists to remember that love has cultural significance. Education will be utterly futile unless it succeeds in creating friendliness and a sense of brotherhood among people, so that they learn how to live together. For if they don't, the ominous and growing rifts in contemporary society will widen. It might be well also for our political positivists who think only in terms of legal justice, military sanctions and national security, that forgiveness has political power. A great share of responsibility for the present day demoralization in human relationships is that hate and vindictiveness have dominated policy in the relationship between human groups. "Enmity" has been rampant.

Concern has been growing, however, over our "sensate" contemporary culture, this culture whose soul has been science and whose interests have been exclusively the spatial and temporal, the visible and the tangible. The Harvard sociologist, Sorokin, has taken the lead in indicting the exclusive devotion to the "sensate," which he regards as today completely exhausted with nothing more to give. But this religious devotion to the things of sense, the things men can *have*, he does not regard as ultimately sinful, but only as contemporaneously harmful. The pursuit of the sensate is not, for Sorokin, the expression of a spiritual aberration; it is rather the manifestation of a cyclical rhythm whose appropriate length has been unduly prolonged in our time. So our great contemporary need, in this professor's view, is to stress the ideational, by which he means devotion to spiritual values. But should the cynic say that such values are objectively unreal and flatly deny the objectivity or propriety of the cultural rhythm, then the "saint," the man who is so committed to ultimate spiritual values that he engages in ascetic discipline, must, according to this view, become our representative type. But it will obviously be a forlorn hope to try to produce saints and promote harbingers of an ideational culture, unless they believe what their sociological advocate does not himself believe, namely, that the values they stand for are absolutely true and are guaranteed by a cosmic order. That is to say, the "saints" who alone can redeem our cultural order cannot be created to order, nor by such presuppositions as Sorokin proposes.

In philosophical circles the deepest kind of concern begins to be expressed over the spiritual chasm that divides the East and the West and separates the great religions of mankind. What is needed, it is maintained, is to transcend the partial and create an overarching loyalty to which all could adhere. Northrop, the Yale philosopher, concludes his book, *The Meeting of East and West: An Essay in Human Understanding,* with a plea for world-loyalty. In the interests of world-loyalty mutuality should be promoted between East and West, each sharing with the other its ideals. But how utterly unreal is such a proposal at a moment in history when the traditional ideals of both East and West are passing away, and when a tremendous force, that of Marxist Communism, proclaims around the world that what matters is not the mutuality of ideals but the common recognition of realities!

In a book which appeared between the two wars, embodying the report of a Commission whose Chairman was the distinguished Harvard philosopher, Professor W. E. Hocking, and entitled *A Laymen's Enquiry Concerning Christian Missions*, the idea was advanced that, in view of what seemed to be an emergent world-culture, the spiritual future of mankind lay in moving towards "the New Testament of every existing Faith." But apart from the fact that a cultural vacuum and not an emergent world-culture is what chiefly marks our western world, the aftermath of the Second World War has witnessed a very decided disintegration of the ancient faiths that dominated the East. Where new developments have recently taken place in Buddhism, Hinduism, and Islam, they are strongly linked to nationalism. They show no interest in an emergent "New Testament."

The Way of Power

The Way of Wisdom, however, has not been the only way in which the attempt has been made to introduce order and unity into human confusion and conflict. Some have tried to do this by the application of force.

Alexander and Augustus were famous representatives in ancient times of the way of power. It was the ambition of one to unite and humanize the vast empire he conquered through the diffusion of Greek culture. The other, believing himself to be the author of the ideal and permanent constitution, set about unifying his wide dominions from the Tiber to "Ultima Thule" by the imposition of Roman Law.

At the dawn of the modern era the sponsors of Columbus, Ferdinand and Isabel of Spain, and the Spanish monarchs who succeeded them in Spain's Golden Age, set about the enforced establishment of a theocracy in the Western World which Columbus had discovered. In practice the indigenous peoples were obliged to do obeisance to the Cross or be disembowelled by the sword. At the close of the modern era, the principles of Democracy, which has been the greatest political achievement of this era, are promoted by force, though it may not be despotic force, among the peoples in the West and in the East who were conquered by the democratic powers in the Second World War.

The ideal of a Theocracy, a divinely inspired pattern of society, which is to be imposed by force, force which shall achieve the totalitarian control of life, outer and inner, of all citizens, continues to be operative in our time. Its representative secular expression is "Hispanidad," its characteristic religious expression is "Clericalism."

"Hispanidad" is the theory which inspires the present fascist rulers of Spain and Argentina. It signifies that the Hispanic race, when guided by the Roman Catholic Church, has the historic mission of showing how a true political paternalism is the best form of government for human beings. The unity which has been established between Church and State in Franco's Spain is one of the most terrifying things in the history of civilization.

Clericalism is the pursuit of power, especially political power, by a religious hierarchy, carried on by secular methods and for purposes of social domination. The supreme expression of Clericalism is Roman Clericalism. The Roman Catholic hierarchy, regarding itself as constituting one true Church of Jesus Christ, believes that it has been given the divine mission to bring society and the State under the complete control of the Church as a visible institution. Only that relationship to the State can be regarded as politically ideal in which the State is willing to accept the viewpoint of the Church on all matters relating to faith and morals, to truth and error. The State shall so exercise its power that individuals and groups regarded by the Church as representing and propagating error shall not enjoy the full rights and privileges of citizens, but be the object of such coercion as may appear desirable to lead them to an acceptance of the established theocratic order. Clericalism is founded upon a low view of Man, even Christian man and his possibilities, and upon an unwarrantable view of the Church as the visible, institutional and authoritative Kingdom of God on earth. It represents, in its contemporary development, an increasing aberration from the Christian religion. It has ceased to be Christ's servant and has become His patron. It is today, as will appear later, one of the most sinister foes of God's Order.

But nothing, not even Roman Clericalism, is so dramatic and world-wide in its endeavor to constitute by force a terrestrial unity, a secular paradise as Marxist Communism. Inspired by the thesis that in the inexorable dialectic of history the hour has struck for Proletarian man to rule the world, under the leadership of the Holy Mother Russia, the first and most potent Communist state, Communism moves across the world with crusading passion and an apocalyptic sense of destiny. Committed to the truth of historical materialism and economic determinism, and regarding all human ideals and religious systems as creations of class interest, which are predestined to pass away with the establishment of a Communist society, Communism tolerates religion when it maintains itself strictly within the sanctuary and persecutes it ruthlessly when it presumes to challenge or influence the secular order. Expert geopoliticians, possessed of the best intelligence system in the world, rejecting all moral standards, confident that the "radiant forces" of history are with them, the rulers of Russia have set out on the greatest imperialistic movement in history to dominate "all nations and peoples and tongues." They take seriously the famous dictum of Sir Halford Mackinder, the innocent source of modern geopolitics, that "who rules Eastern Europe commands the Heartland; who rules the Heartland commands the World-Island; who rules the World-Island commands the world." Communist Russia, secure in that vast region of Europe and Asia which in winter is covered with snow, proceeds to the conquest of the World-Island, Europe, Asia and Africa. Then, unless the New Imperialism is frustrated, will follow world dominion and the iron reign of Antichrist!

But there is an Order of God, as well as an order of man. And God is the Lord! In the background of the Great Rift with its implications and consequences and the human attempts to solve the world's disorder without reference to the true source of its woes, we pass to consider the Great Unveiling.

CHAPTER III

God's Unveiled Secret

What is God's solution of the problem, human and cosmic, created by the Rift? What is the Divine approach to the quest of Unity which so many "desperate imperialisms" of wisdom and power have tried to achieve in history and still strive to achieve in our time? Let Paul be our guide as we follow his thought through the Ephesian Letter.

a) ITS APOSTOLIC MEDIUM

We first pause on the threshold of the Epistle to hear how he introduces himself to the wide ecumenical constituency whom he addresses. He is "Paul an Apostle of Christ Jesus by the will of God." As an "apostle" he is one who was called and commissioned by Jesus Christ Himself. His special title to apostleship is, as he informs us in other writings, that he had "seen the Lord" and had "heard his voice" and received His personal word of command. He knew the meaning of the will of God, because God had willed to "reveal His Son in him" (Gal. 1:16). He was a man who had been "separated unto the Gospel of God" (Rom. 1:1). Paul thus clearly regarded himself to be an apostle of Jesus Christ in a very particular sense. He was not only entrusted with the message of the Gospel, as were the other apostles, but God had willed that the full implications of the Gospel, which he calls the "Mystery," should be made known to him "by revelation" (Eph. 3:3). God, that is to say, had constituted him a very special apostle, a "steward" or "executor" of a revelation, until then hidden, of the full range of God's purpose in relation to the world and to man. He who had been "born out of due time," who, in his own estimate of himself, was "less than the least of all the saints" (3:8) and "not worthy to be called an apostle," led the apostolic van in his experience and grasp of the innermost intent and cosmic outreach of the "will of God."

It was, therefore, out of a humbling experience of God's condescension to himself and a deep insight into the vastness of the divine mercy to mankind, that Paul invoked "grace" and "peace" upon those who, like himself, had become "saints," people separated unto God by their faith in Jesus Christ. Let grace, God's unmerited favor, and His peace that brings inward unity to the soul, flow to them from the Father everlasting and from their Lord Jesus Christ.

Identification and greeting over, a rapturous flight carries the writer into the heart of the "vision splendid." He mounts into the empyrean where takes place the great Unveiling. No passage in the Bible combines music, grandeur and momentous import in the same measure that the next twelve verses do (1:3–14). I cannot do better than transcribe at this point the description of these verses which had been given by a man who, more than any other in his time, entered into the spirit of the Ephesian Letter: "The twelve verses which follow baffle our analysis. They are a kaleidoscope of dazzling lights and shifting colours. At first we fail to find a trace of order or method. They are like the preliminary flight of the eagle, rising and wheeling round, as though for a while uncertain what direction in his boundless freedom he shall take. So the Apostle's thought lifts itself beyond the limits of time and above the material conceptions that confine ordinary men, and ranges this way and that in a region of spirit, a heavenly sphere with no course as yet marked out, merely exulting in the attributes and purposes of God. . . . He seems to be swept along by his theme, hardly knowing where it is taking him. He begins with God, the blessing which comes from God to men, the eternity of his purpose of good, the glory of its consummation. But he cannot order his conception or close his sentences. One thought presses hard upon another, and will not be refused. And so this great doxology runs on and on: in whom—in Him—, in Him—, in whom—in—in whom—. But as we read it again and again we begin to perceive certain great words recurring and revolving round a central point: The will of God working itself out to some glorious issue in Christ, that is his theme. A single phrase of the ninth verse sums it up: it is 'the mystery of His will.' " [1]

b) DIVINE OVERTURE

The reality of the sovereign and gracious God anchors Paul's thought. It also enlarges his heart and makes his imagination glow. He offers no rival interpretation of the Universe in opposition to the theories current in his time. He does not descant upon the superiority of the Christian religion over its rivals. He does not argue for God against all "agonized attempts to deny Him." He affirms, he proclaims; rather he adores. With an act of adoration, "Blessed be the God and Father of our Lord Jesus Christ, who has blessed us in Christ with every spiritual blessing in the heavenly places," he begins to speak.

It was suggested in the chapter on *Perspectives* that this rhapsodic adoration is comparable to the overture of an opera which contains the successive melodies that are to follow. That is true. This is the bugle note, the sounding of reveille at daybreak. The

---
[1] J. Armitage Robinson, *op. cit.*, p. 19.

darkness is past; a program of dramatic happenings is to be announced. The hidden counsels of Deity have become an open secret. Heaven has come to earth. The proof is that a multitude of people, among whom Paul includes himself, have the witness in themselves that a new order of life has come. They have been actually blessed "with every spiritual blessing in the heavenly places." Not that they had experienced the full range of this "spiritual blessing," but they had the Holy Spirit in their lives (1:14), and He was the guarantee that eventually they would understand, and participate in, the full range of blessing. Let them, therefore, bless God who had so mightily blessed them. He who had bestowed inexhaustible benefits upon men was worthy of an inexhaustible ascription of praise from men.

God: What was present in Paul's mind and heart when in an ecstasy of adoration he called upon himself and all the "saints" to "bless" God, to ascribe blessedness to "the God and Father of our Lord Jesus Christ"?

The Pharisee "baptized unto Christ" had in his religious heritage the majestic view of God that inspired Moses and the Prophets. His God was the God of Israel who was also the God of the whole earth. He, whom in another Letter written from his Roman prison Paul calls "my God" (Phil. 4:19), was the living God. He was not one among many divinities who could thwart His action. His freedom was not bound by cosmic fate. He was not a construct of men's minds, nor could He be described by any synthetic attempt to fuse together attributes regarded as divine. God could be known only by His works, by what He had done and was doing. Apart from His activity He could not be known at all. He was always subject, never object. Of Him who in the Old Testament spoke of Himself as "I am," it could only be said, "*God is.*" And this God who eternally *is*, in as much as He is not the product of the human mind nor is dependent upon human action, can neither be patronized, nor bargained with, nor be made an instrument of human policy. He is as little the God of politicians and world-rulers as of the Pascalian "philosophers and scholars."

But the God of Paul, while He is sovereign in His majesty, is much more than pure might, infinitely more than arbitrary power. He is a God concerned about men and gracious towards men. Unlike the God of Aristotle, his thinking is not done merely upon thought. He has more than an aesthetic interest in the world. The God of the Ephesian Letter is no mere summer tourist for whom men are only scenery.[2] God's concern is expressed by Paul in the Epistle to the Romans, the greatest of his writings before he wrote his Letter to the Ephesians. There God appears as being in a very special sense the "God of Abraham." His concern for men led Him to "call" Abraham, to make a "covenant" with the patriarch from Ur. Abraham "believed" God. At God's command this Chaldee, who dwelt by the Euphrates in an advanced center of civilization, became imbued with a divine "concern." Though far beyond the modern age of retirement, and enjoying the eventide detachment from life which Aristotle in his *Ethics* regarded as a trait of human blessedness, he took off his slippers and put on his shoes for an adventurous journey into the Unknown. He became an alien in a strange land, starting life afresh as a colonist in a place where nomad shepherds tended their flocks. Taking God seriously when He promised he would have a son who should be a man of destiny, to carry forward God's concern to bless mankind, Abraham set about raising a family. As the "father of the faithful," the pioneer of a new order, Abraham became for the converted Pharisee in his Roman prison the man who, of all who lived before Christ came, expressed most perfectly what can with reverence be called God's adventurous concern for the human kind. For the aged Chaldee exile in the Palestinean plateau was in the events of his life the symbol and embodiment of that frontier spirit, that purposive advance into the future, which has marked the God of the Bible and the lives of all godlike men.

---
[2] W. H. Auden.

The God of Abraham became revealed to mankind in the "fullness of time" as the God and Father of Jesus Christ. God as the Father of the sons of Abraham, that is of the Hebrew people, becomes the Father of a Person. That Person is in a unique sense His Son. That Son proclaimed, as it had never been proclaimed before, that God was supremely Father.

Behind the screen of appearance, controlling the movement of history, underlying cosmic mystery, there is a Father. The recognition that the Ultimate Reality in the universe is paternal, that the Fatherhood of God is true, that the fact of Christ was the proof and pattern of Divine Fatherhood, moved Paul to hurl his heart into a paean. We may well pause a moment to ponder what it really means to believe that there is an Almighty Father in the Universe. Really to believe this and to feel it, is to exult, as Paul exulted, that the Universe is not a vast machine. Laws there are in it; efficient action is a mark of it; inexorable and ruthless processes are not absent from it; but the attributes of mechanism at its best do not exhaust what the Universe is. A Father's will controls the machine, which is the work of His infinite wisdom and the instrument of His paternal purpose. That will and that purpose are superior to physical necessity. They are not bound by any dialectic or determinism of history. Because God is Father the world is not an orphanage. If it were, the terrestrial human kindness which we know would have no ultimate divine goodness to correspond to it. Men would be like disillusioned orphans waking up to the fact of their cosmic solitariness. Because God is Father, still less is human history a vast cemetery of dead values. A cemetery can be a place of entrancing beauty, but aesthetic loveliness is poor compensation for immortal hope. But there *is* a Father. The ultimate spiritual pattern is that of a paternal Kingdom. Therefore, might is not right. Souls are not for sale. Fatherhood among men, and all that it signifies, is grounded upon the reality of a Divine universal Fatherhood. And the glory of this Fatherhood is, as Paul suggests, that the universal Father is also the archetypal Father. For God is "the Father of whom all fatherhood is named" (Eph. 3:14, 15). All that is noblest in human affection has its source in, and is patterned upon, the Fatherhood of God.

This fatherly God is the God and Father of "our Lord Jesus Christ." Paul, so far as we know, never saw Jesus of Nazareth in the flesh. It is said he was not interested in the early life of Christ, because he is largely silent about it. It is true that, when he refers to the historical Figure it is to relate Him to the Divine Being "who humbled Himself, took upon Him the form of a servant, and became obedient unto death" (Phil. 2:8) and who was by the great power of God raised from the dead. But let us remember that it was not Paul's task to write another life of Christ, to vie with those of his travelling companions, Mark and Luke. His task was to proclaim the relationship of Jesus of Nazareth to the pre-existent Christ, and to set forth the significance for Israel and the Church, for mankind and for the cosmos, of the Risen Christ who had called him to be His Apostle. And yet we cannot escape the tender interest which Paul had in the Man of Galilee. He adds another item to the collection of Jesus' teachings as recorded in the Gospels, when (according to Acts 20:35) he introduces on one occasion "the words of the Lord Jesus," "It is more blessed to give than to receive." But more important than that is the fact that Paul's own teaching on the great spiritual issues is, as the most recent New Testament study has pointed out, virtually identical with that of Jesus. Not only so, but his own life as a "servant of Jesus Christ" comes closer than that of any Christian who ever lived to Him whose great glory was that He "humbled Himself and took upon Him the form of a servant." No one can escape the evidence of the measure in which the "mind of Christ" was in Paul and that the concrete life of Jesus was as normative for his thinking about God and man as it is intended to be for all Christians.

The really important thing is to recognize that the man called

Jesus was for Paul, as He was for the early Christians, the Messiah of Israel, the Son of God Incarnate, who had been sent by God upon a mission of redemptive mercy, who was like God in His life, in whose sufferings and death God was present, and whom God raised again from the dead and exalted to the chief seat of universal power. When Paul and the early Christians formulated that first and most basic creed: "Jesus Christ is Lord" (Phil. 2:11), they applied to Jesus a term which in the Septuagint was used of Jehovah the God of Israel, and was used among the Romans to designate imperial Caesar. The God, the thought of whom sent Paul into a rhapsody, was the God whose nature as the eternal Father was set forth supremely in the life, teaching, death, resurrection and exaltation of Jesus Christ the Lord, and whose sovereign and most gracious purpose became manifest in and through Jesus Christ. This was so, both because of what Jesus Christ did, and because the "faithful in Christ Jesus" were blessed by God "with every spiritual blessing in the heavenly places."

The full magnitude and implications of this "blessing" are the theme of what immediately follows this magnificent overture. At this point let it suffice to say before we pass on to the concrete unveiling of the Divine purpose, that "every spiritual blessing in the heavenly places," as Paul conceives it, includes and carries forward all that is meant in the Synoptic Gospels by the "Kingdom of God," the "new age" and its blessings which came with power in Jesus Christ. It includes what Paul himself meant in the Letter to the Romans by the "Righteousness from God," that new order of existence which came into the world with, and is mediated to the souls of men through, Jesus Christ.

With this we are ready to consider the vast scheme of reconciliation, God's fatherly, redemptive will to unity, which he purposed in Christ, whereby the power of love triumphed where the love of power failed.

c) THE "MYSTERY OF HIS WILL"

The burden of Paul's message to the Christians scattered throughout the Roman world was that the secret of God's purpose, hitherto hidden from all mankind, had now been revealed. It was the object of his ecumenical letter to inform them that light had been flashed into the darkness of man's estate and that the tragic enigma of human life had been solved by a Divine Unveiling. This unveiling, or rather the Unveiled Secret, he called the "Mystery." He, Paul, had been constituted by God the "steward" or "executor" of this "Mystery" to make known to all men its "plan," "the plan of the mystery hidden for ages in God who created all things" (Eph. 3:9). His fulfillment of this special function as the "Executor" who was charged to see to it that the knowledge of the "Mystery" was diffused throughout the world, Paul related closely to his office as a "Minister of the Gospel," whom God had set apart "to preach to the Gentiles the unsearchable riches of Christ" (3:7, 8). For him and for his apostolic mission, the "Mystery," the "Gospel" and "Christ" are all inseparably bound up together.

Some observations are appropriate, before we go further, regarding the term "Mystery" as here used by St. Paul. It is important to bear in mind that his use of the term has nothing to do with modern usage. We mean by "Mystery," something strange, inscrutable, enigmatic, something which needs to be unravelled and for which a clue is needed. So we speak about "mystery stories." Paul meant by "Mystery" just the opposite from what we do. For him a "mystery" was a hidden secret which had been revealed. The "Mystery," therefore, was "the open secret," a supremely important Divine truth, which God had before held secret but which He had now made known.

It is natural that some connection should be sought between Paul's interest in the "Mystery" and the "Mystery" cults which were current in his time. The breakdown of the old religions of Greece was accompanied by the invasion of oriental cults. With the disintegration of traditional structures of religious faith and social custom, and the growth of a sceptical enquiring spirit, men then as now began to feel an intense spiritual loneliness. They were thrown back on themselves and were ready for all sorts of religious experimentation. The "Mystery" cult was a kind of "Free-Masonry." Following appropriate purification and sacramental rites the devotees were initiated into certain esoteric knowledge and given the promise of immortality. But the "Mystery" of which Paul was the "executor" did not call for the initiation of a special few into what was esoteric. It called for the proclamation to all men of what had been unveiled and made public, and which, on that account, had the status of common knowledge. Those initiated into the "mysteries" were pledged not to reveal the secrets of the cult; Christians were pledged to pass on the "Open Secret."

There is no evidence that Paul's use of the term "Mystery" owed even the name to the prevailing cults. It appears rather that he derived it from purely Jewish sources. In the "Book of Enoch," for example, which had long been lost, and of which large portions have now been restored, the word "mystery" is used repeatedly of "divine secrets which rightly or wrongly have come to the knowledge of man." On the other hand, there is little doubt that Paul, with his keen sensitivity to human situations, very deliberately used a term which was currently in vogue and infused into it a new and challenging content.

Three phases of the "Mystery" are set forth in the Ephesian Letter. The first is the *vertical* phase. God "has made known to us," says Paul, "in all wisdom and insight the mystery of His will, according to His purpose which He sets forth in Christ, as a plan for the fullness of time, to unite all things in Him, things in heaven and things on earth" (1:9, 10). This means that God has constituted Jesus Christ the unifying center of a vast scheme of unity whereby the celestial and terrestrial orders, separated as they now are by the great gulf between the supernatural and the natural, and the greater gulf between the holy and the sinful, shall be joined together in a united Commonwealth. In this transcendental unity in which all God's creation shall be "summed up in Christ," God's will shall be done perfectly. His kingdom will have come in the fullest sense. The Rift will have been totally overcome.

The second phase may be designated the *horizontal* or the *historical* phase. As a prelude to the horizontal unity, the greatest rift that history has known, the rift between Jews and Gentiles, shall be healed. This healing also takes place in Christ. It is Paul's task, as he regards it, to proclaim "the Mystery of Christ," into which he has special insight, according to which "the Gentiles are fellow-heirs, members of the same body, and partakers of the promise in Christ Jesus by the Gospel" (3:4-6). The constitution of a single human family, among people historically alienated from one another, is made possible, because, as we shall see later, Jesus Christ destroyed the "enmity," the "hostility" that kept them apart. Jew and Gentile became reconciled to one another because both became reconciled to God. Through Christ they became members of the same Body: the new man, the new humanity, the new Israel, which is constituted by the Christian Church. The meaning clearly is that God proposes to relate to Himself in one great family people whom historical hates, cultural differences, social status, have held apart. The unifier is Jesus Christ and the unifying principle is the "Gospel."

The third phase of the "Mystery" is that, as a result of the transforming and unifying action of the Church in history, spirits, both good and evil, who are higher than human spirits, shall by contemplating this churchly activity obtain their deepest insight into the wisdom, the "many-coloured wisdom," of God (3:10). There is no sublimer thought in the Ephesian Letter or in all Scripture than this. The history of the Christian Church becomes a graduate school for angels. By studying the Body of

Christ intelligences superior to man receive new flashes of insight into the divine nature. They come to understand things which had been to them inscrutable in God's dealings with men, and they catch a vision of the ultimate splendor and dimensions of the Creator's purpose in Christ. And what they contemplate is not that kind of wisdom which consists in grasping ideas that were always there; they behold the operation of power that becomes the source of new ideas. For the power that works in the Church and the wisdom made manifest in the operations of that power, far outstrip in significance all the secular manifestations of wisdom and power which man has used to deal with the problem of a rifted universe.

God's will to unity is thus the most central thing in cosmic and human history. This Divine drive none dare ignore, for whatever man attempts that runs counter to it will ultimately be frustrated and shattered by it. As for Christians it is important that they explore in the fullest degree the nature and implications of this unity which God pursues, this order of life which He is establishing.

What is the nature of this unity which is achieved by God's power and is supremely expressive of His wisdom? The unity which God wills is a *religious unity*. A religious unity is a unity in which created spirits live in perfect harmony with the will of the Creator. This is the only kind of unity which has any meaning in the thought of the Bible. It is this unity which is central in Paul's thinking and which constitutes the great theme of the Ephesian Letter. The great problem of mankind is not to achieve intellectual clarity in interpreting the Universe. The problem, that is to say, is not philosophical. Nor is it political, to find some principle of expediency or compromise which shall constitute a work-a-day agreement among men. Still less is it an aesthetic problem, to introduce such beauty into the portrayal of the Universe that men shall forget its ugliness, or to produce through certain artistic creations a catharsis of human emotion which shall immunize man from concern about the world's tragedy. The real problem is to constitute a spiritual unity in which men, being united in their loyalty to God, shall be loyally devoted to one another.

Such a unity is not an abstract unity. It is a community, a fellowship of human spirits who are united to God and to one another. What God wills, therefore, is not mere unity, but community. And the community which God wills is not a class-less society such as the Marxists look forward to, which would express the ultimate goal of Evolution, but be entirely lacking in spiritual dimension. The community which God wills is a fellowship of love, constituted not by an evolution in history, but by the intervention of God in history. It is a community constituted by Jesus Christ, who by what He was and did brought God and man and man and man together in love. In this community love is designed to be regnant and the hierarchical principle, that of reverence for true superiority, is designed to be real. The true finality of history, therefore, the supreme objective which God wills, is not the triumph of wisdom in a guild of scholars, nor the victory of power in a fascist oligarchy, nor yet the imposition of a communistic class-less society from which hierarchical allegiance would be excluded. God's will to fellowship seeks a community of love, an order of life in which He would reign in every human heart and in every human relationship.

It is obvious, however, that such a community can be constituted only by a change in human nature. Marx was right when he maintained, against traditional philosophy, that the real task is not to think the world but to change it. He was wrong when he considered that mere change in the structure and constitution of human society was itself the revolutionary event that was needed. Marx was not radical, not revolutionary enough. The real change that needs to be achieved, the change that the will of God invincibly pursues, is to change man from self-centeredness and class-centeredness into God-centeredness. But this means, not revolution but salvation. It means redemption, the deliverance of man from the power and effects of his rebellious, self-seeking, god-making will. Community, in the fullest sense, salvation in the completest sense, are eschatological in character, that is, they can be realized fully only at the end of history as we know it. But until "righteousness and peace kiss mutually," until God sets up "His Kingdom which cannot be shaken," two things will be true. The first is this: the presence of love, working in a limited community of love, will be the supremely creative and preservative force in human society. And the second: "The Gospel of your salvation," which is also the "Gospel of the glory of the blessed God," both in its verbal proclamation and its vital expression, will be the chief concern of all who know the "Mystery" and live by it.

d) LOVE EVERLASTING AND INVINCIBLE

It is now necessary to consider the force that moves the Divine will to fellowship, God's purpose to constitute in Christ a "Commonwealth of Heaven and Earth," which is unveiled in the "Mystery." That force is love, the holy, sovereign, passionate love of God. The love of God is the driving power behind the cosmic and historical movement towards spiritual unity.

The love of God, which occupies so central a place in the Epistle to the Ephesians, and which constitutes the central theme of the Bible as a whole, is a passionate concern for and devotion to people who are not naturally lovely or loveable, who are in themselves essentially unworthy and sinful. It is *agape*, God's way to man whereby he yearns over man, seeks his good, strives to deliver him from his sinful rebellion, becomes his Saviour and makes him His son. This love is something totally different from what the Greeks called *Eros*. Eros was an aspiration after and devotion to all natural loveliness and beauty. In the presence of the ugly, the unworthy, the sinful and the derelict, Eros was out of place; it could inspire no passion or concern.

God, says Paul, thinking of the people who were "dead in trespasses and sins," lustful in their bodies and futile in their minds, living without hope and alienated from God, "destined us in love to be His sons through Jesus Christ" (Eph. 1:5). He wooed such people into interests and attitudes which they did not naturally have; He gave them a status which they did not naturally deserve. When, therefore, God made lost men His "sons," sonship was a gift given to sinners and not a crown bestowed upon victors.

But the love of God towards the men whom He made His "sons" did not begin in history nor in the lifetime of His "sons." He "chose" them in Christ "before the foundation of the world"; He "destined," or "predestined," them to be "sons" "according to the purpose of His will" (1:5).

We approach here a very great and important question, a question about which, in some epochs, bitter controversies raged in the Christian Church. It is the question of God's Election or of Divine Predestination. It is important that we devote some attention to this matter. The context of the Ephesian Letter is a good setting in which to consider it, and the issue involved is one of basic interest and concern. In fact, the general problem of the philosophy of history and the particular problem of historical determinism give very great actuality to the whole question of what may be called the Election of Grace.

The essential problem, of course, is this. How shall a great spiritual purpose be infallibly, or if you like, inexorably achieved, in history, without human freedom being violated? How shall a Divine or cosmic goal be attained in the world of men, in which the destiny and cooperation of men are involved, without those men being automata, that is to say, without their being mere pawns in a game the conclusion of which does not depend upon their volition? Such a problem is as much a problem for philosophy as it is for religion.

Let us examine first the conception of freedom. When are men truly free? Men are not free when their action is determined by a mere whim or caprice. In such a case the whim or caprice is their master. Men are not free when an authority of some kind forces them to do something whose essential rightness or importance is not apparent to them. In true freedom two conditions must be fulfilled. One is the universal validity or worth of what one is asked to accept; the second is the personal voluntariness with which one is able to act. Such freedom is reflected in the lines of the hymn, "Make me a captive, Lord, and then I shall be free." This is a recognition of the fact that true freedom is a submission to the Divine. There is no serfdom involved when the human spirit becomes the voluntary joyous agent of the Infinite and the Holy. "I would fain be to the Eternal Goodness what his own hand is to a man." There you have an exuberant aspiration to be the voluntary yet inevitable agent of God's gracious purposes.

Here is a matter in which the Marxists show great insight. For the Marxist, freedom consists in "recognizing a superior necessity." This superior necessity is of course "Economic Determinism" and the whole world-view which is bound up with it. But the important thing to remember is that no true Communist regards himself to be a serf. He is fulfilling, even when he submits to the iron yoke of dictatorship, an inevitable, though, as he hopes, temporary expression, of the "radiant forces of the Universe." How much more gloriously free is a man who, when admitted into sonship in God's family, accepts the yoke that God imposes to promote the father's will to fellowship, and so to enjoy the "glorious liberty of the children of God"?

But the chief difficulty in the minds of some is that an "Election of Grace" or "predestinating love" would appear to involve an arbitrary selection on God's part of some favored folk to the exclusion of others. Let it be observed that Paul introduces the idea of God's Election "before the foundation of the world" in order to explain to the "saints" to whom he wrote how it came about that they had the experience which they did. What had happened to them was not casual. Their new hope in Christ was not illusion; for their life and destiny were embraced by an eternal plan of God which was working itself out in them. God had thought of them before they were born and before even the worlds were made. Therefore, let them be of good courage. It was as if Paul would teach them each one to say to God:

"Thou wast beforehand with my soul
Ever Thou lovest me."

It should be borne in mind also that John Calvin, who is associated in many minds with a view of Divine predestination which has an arbitrary ring to it, does not introduce this doctrine until he reaches the third book of his *Institutes of the Christian Religion*. When he does it is not in connection with his doctrine of God, but with his doctrine of the Christian man. Like Paul, he relates God's Election to the Christian experience of regeneration as its ultimate antecedent. In his Children's Catechism this doctrine, regarded by Calvin as strong meat for those of full age, does not appear at all. It was only as a result of bitter controversy over the divine plan of salvation that the doctrine of Predestination took on the prominence in Calvin's thought which is associated with his name. Protestant scholasticism of a later day did what Calvin never did: it dealt with Predestination in discussing the doctrine of God.

But here we are dealing with Paul and the Ephesian Letter. So far as Paul's thought in this the maturest of his writings is concerned, these are the salient facts: The "Saints" whom he addressed were chosen "in love." Now love can think no evil nor do evil. Where love, therefore, is the power behind selection, the fatalism of necessity and the arbitrariness of power are both excluded. Where love is supreme there is no place for fate or caprice.

They were moreover "chosen in Christ" (1:4); God ordained that Jesus Christ should be both the Saviour of men and the center of all spiritual unity both in time and beyond time. Christ was not a mere instrument of the Divine election; men were chosen in Him and for Him. Karl Barth is entirely right when, in his reinterpretation of the classical doctrine of Predestination, making it both more scriptural and so more Christian, he affirms that there is no absolute divine decree apart from Jesus Christ. Paradoxically speaking, Christ is both the electing God and the elected Man. To be "chosen in Christ," means, therefore, to be chosen to be saved by one who excludes no one who comes to Him. None are cut off from God's election in Christ but those who deliberately cut themselves off.

But Paul and his readers were also chosen to be "holy and blameless." God willed that they should be truly like Jesus Christ in whom they were chosen. Woe betide them if they were ever to think that they should "sin that grace might abound," or that anything other than goodness was the fruit which God sought in their lives. Their Christlikeness was not to be made manifest merely in spiritual inwardness and passive virtues. They were chosen by God for "good works," of a visible and outward nature. That is to say, God chose men not to make them pampered children, Christian Pharisees or intolerable prigs. He wanted people who would do His "works" and carry forward His work.

In a word, they were chosen to the "praise of His glory" (Eph. 1:12). The great finality of the everlasting and invincible love of God was to form men who would be truly godlike, men, that is to say, who would aspire to godlikeness in God and with God. It would be their constant ambition to "glorify" God, that is, to make Him manifest in their words and their deeds, striving to be "perfect as their Father in Heaven is perfect."

e) THE HISTORICAL ORGAN OF AN ETERNAL PURPOSE

Leaving for special consideration in the next chapter the reality of Jesus Christ as the Creator and center of all spiritual unity in human and cosmic history, let us consider, at the close of this chapter, the organ which God designated to give historical fulfillment to the "plan of the Mystery."

That organ is a community, the community of the "chosen in Christ," of the "destined in love." This community may be called generally "The People of God." In the Epistle to the Ephesians, which is supremely interested in the corporate side of Christianity, the "People of God" occupy a central place. In the Old Testament they formed the "Commonwealth of Israel"; in the New Testament the Christian Church, the "Body of Christ."

God's purpose to create a new humanity, and to constitute a spiritual unity on a grander scale than that which had been rifted, led in the course of human history to the choice of a special nation to become the organ of his redemptive will. In choosing a man, Abraham, to become the ancestor of a "chosen race" God did two things. He deepened the rift between peoples, so that the awareness of this choice on the part of the "children of Abraham" became the source of the most bitter racial cleavage of which history has record. On the other hand, a nation was formed which God designed, by an experience of redemption, and a special process of education, to be the collective medium for furthering His eternal purpose. A people without political greatness or native religious genius became the "People of God."

The "Commonwealth of Israel," to use Paul's designation (Eph. 2:12), manifested throughout its history two main characteristics. The Hebrew people had an intense awareness of the reality of God, and an equally intense awareness of their own destiny under God. They had a sense of Presence and a sense of Destiny. As the "People of the Presence" they were a people whose whole history received its meaning from a consciousness of the Divine nearness. God spoke to them; He called them; He led them. In their wilderness wanderings He dwelt between the "Cherubim of glory" which surrounded "The Sacred Ark of the Covenant." They struck their tents to follow Him when He moved forward in a Cloud or a Fiery Pillar. "O Lord, show me Thy glory [thine unveiled splendor]," said the Lawgiver of Israel. And again: "If Thy Presence go not with us, carry us not up hence" (Ex. 33:15).

Israel had an equal sense of Destiny. They knew that God had made them a nation and controlled their national life for a purpose. That purpose was to bless the world. The pages of the Psalms and of the Prophets glow with visions of the coming Messianic Kingdom. A great Deliverer, a Messianic King, was to come to Israel who would overcome all the enemies of God's people and make Israel the Nation of Destiny.

This dual sense of Presence and Destiny gave to the "Commonwealth of Israel" an extraordinary, an unprecedented, unity. Israel had *one God,* Jehovah the Lord God of Israel, who had made a Covenant with His people, who was also the "God of all the earth." Israel had *one Law.* Upon obedience to that *Law* God's presence with His people and the destiny of Israel depended. Israel had *one Holy City,* Jerusalem, the "City of the Great King," which was literally the center of the earth, the true world capital to which all nations would one day come to "worship the King, the Lord of Hosts." Israel had *one Temple.* The Temple at Jerusalem was not only the center of Israel's worship, it was also, as Jewish writers regard it, the "navel of the earth." That is to say, through the temple, the earth received or was to receive, its spiritual nourishment.

But Israel lost the Presence and failed to fulfill its Destiny. A moment came in Israel's history when the nation, spiritually blinded, failed to recognize its Messiah and refused to undertake the next step needful to bless the world. The nation in its pride desired to be blessed rather than to bless. It wanted to have rather than to be. It was more interested in receiving security from God than in rendering service to God. It had lost the pilgrim sense; it balked at a great new adventure such as Abraham undertook in leaving Babylonia, such as Moses undertook in leaving Egypt, such as the great Prophets of Israel envisaged as the coming role of Israel. So the Messiah was crucified; a new People of God was constituted and the Commonwealth of Israel ceased to be spiritually significant for the unfolding of the Eternal Purpose.

The Christian Church, in whose membership the antagonism between Jew and Gentile is transcended and overcome, because God has reconciled them both to Himself "in one body," is the New Israel. It is more than that, it is the New Man, the New Humanity (Eph. 2:15). Thus the unity of the Church is not a question of practical Church politics or statesmanship. Those who have "been brought near, in the blood of Christ" (2:13), who have been "reconciled to God through the Cross" (2:16), who have "access in one Spirit to the Father" (2:18), who "are a dwelling place of God in the Spirit" (2:22), who form the "Church, which is His Body," constitute an ontological unity. That is to say, the Christian Church, as Paul expounds its meaning in the Ephesian Letter, *is* a unity, a collective personality. Its members, through their common relationship to Jesus Christ, have been taken out of one community and placed in another.

We shall have occasion to consider in subsequent chapters Paul's description of the individual member of the new community and of the community as a whole. Suffice it to say regarding the Church, in concluding this chapter, that in the "eternal purpose" of God the Christian Church is designed to be the pattern community in history, and, at the same time, to bless the whole historical community of mankind. In the life and activity of the Church as the New Humanity nothing must ever be allowed to appear in word or deed that is unworthy of the spirit of love which should be regnant within it, in which it is "rooted and grounded" (Eph. 3:17). It cannot be an end in itself because it is the "Body of Christ," the organ of His redemptive will. It must never allow itself to become complacent or aspire to become a kingdom of this world. Surrounded by hostile forces it must never cease to be militant, panoplied "with the whole armor of God." It can never be completely at home in any one form of human society, but it should strive to bless all society. In moments of historical crisis it should be prepared, in order to be loyal to God, to give up everything and become an alien like Abraham, to take up its Cross and follow the Crucified.

Unlike the revolutionary proletariat the Church will not regard itself as the fulfillment of the forces immanent in history; it will view itself rather as the historical organ of a purpose which lies beyond history. A colony of heaven, the Christian Church will, nevertheless, be the decisive community in transforming the earth and in shaping the destiny of those who inhabit it.

As the great Drama proceeds and the Eternal Purpose unfolds, the Christian Church, the New Humanity, becomes the great object lesson by whose study, as we have seen, the "Principalities and Powers in the heavenly places" become schooled in the wisdom of God. The rulers of men might do well also to study this community with the same absorbing interest that the higher spirits do. They will find that the history of the Church holds important lessons for statecraft. Perchance as statesmen or soldiers they will learn to "kiss the Son," to humble themselves before the one and only Victor that history has known. For, at the last, He, and He alone, must reign.

With this let us move on to the most crucial part of our study. Let us consider the role played by Jesus Christ. For He it was who mediated to mankind the Everlasting and Invincible Love of God. He it was who created a New Humanity in which the ancient rift would be healed. It is through Christ that the eternal purpose of God must be fulfilled, in whose fulfillment rhapsodic melody shall send its strains through all the corridors of Time—and of Eternity.

CHAPTER IV

The Victory Which Christ Wrought

The moment we consider the relation of the Christian religion to human thought we come face to face with a great paradox.

a) FAITH'S CORE AND CLUE: A PERSON

The religion which more than any other of the great religions of mankind gave birth to ideas and influenced systems of ideas was not itself a religion of ideas, but the religion of a Person. In the affirmation, "Christianity is Christ," there is something which goes far beyond devout sentiment and theological daring. Jesus Christ is the core of the Christian religion. He is its historical creator as a world faith; He is the center of its religious message; He is also the clue whereby that message, as enshrined in Holy Scripture, can be understood.

St. Paul, in the Ephesian Letter, goes even further than this. The erstwhile bitter foe of Jesus of Nazareth and of the religion which He founded, presents Jesus Christ as the Creator and Center of a new divine order. The Person whom Paul elsewhere calls "my Lord" (Phil. 3:8), about whom he used the words, "who loved me and gave himself for me" (Gal. 2:20), the one who constituted his very life (Gal. 2:20), is set forth as the supreme spiritual conqueror who becomes the foundation and center of God's vast scheme of reconciliation. Confronted with the fact of bitter conflict, of tragic estrangement in history and in his own soul, Paul finds the complete solution of the Great Rift and all its baleful consequences in God's redemptive plan in Jesus Christ.

To every semblance of estrangement in nature and in history Hegel, the great prophet of Absolute Idealism, found the answer in the affirmation that "the rational is the real." In his view the irrational, so-called sin and evil, has no true reality. Karl Marx found the solution of human estrangement, which he identified with the class struggle, in the affirmation that the common people, the disinherited proletariat, when they become revolutionary, fulfill a messianic mission and constitute what is ultimately real. But for Paul, Jesus Christ engaged in conflict to end conflict. The Crucified Figure who became history's most famous center of strife represented God's concerted effort, the "Power of God and the wisdom of God," to bring estrangement to a close between Himself and man and between man and his neighbor. It is not therefore disinherited men who become revolutionary, and assume absolute and divine prerogatives in order to achieve peace and unity, that is the answer to the problem of human disorder. The answer is found rather in the God who humbled himself, who became man, the most disinherited of men, that out of his poverty men "might become rich," and that through His dereliction they might become "sons of God."

For the manifestation of these "sons of God," all creation groaned and travailed in the first century (Rom. 8:22); with even deeper and more reasoned anguish, men and nature groan in this our time, awaiting ampler and worthier fruits of the Victory which Christ wrought.

Let us turn, therefore, to consider the Redeemer of Mankind and the Victory which He accomplished.

b) A LIFE DESTINED FOR DEATH

Who was the Figure whom Paul in the Ephesian Letter designates "Christ," "Christ Jesus" or "our Lord Jesus Christ"? Even though Paul did not, as we have already stated, make much reference to the "Jesus of History," nor ground his "Gospel" upon anything ordinarily associated with His "life," "teaching" or "personality," the whole synoptic tradition regarding Jesus was well known to the man from Tarsus. Paul's great concern, it is true, was with the fact that Jesus was born, that He died, that He rose again from the dead, and that God "highly exalted Him." But while no Form Criticism, nor any form of radicalism in handling the details of Jesus' life, affects Paul's essential position regarding Jesus Christ, the historical Figure and the narrative regarding Him were part of his cherished inheritance from those who had known the "Lord" in the days of His flesh.

Jesus, which means "Saviour," was this Person's name, and "to save" was His mission. He came that He might "save His people from their sins," that is, from having come short of God's mark for their lives, for having missed their true destiny. It would appear that before Jesus of Nazareth, the only private individual to be given the Greek title of *soter* ("savior") was the Hellenic philosopher Epicurus. "That title," says Toynbee, "was normally a monopoly of princes and a reward for political and military services!" But the "unruffled imperturbability" for which Epicurus was famous, and because of which he was greatly loved and revered by his contemporaries in an age of anxiety, did not make him in his time, nor has it made him since, an effective savior of his fellow-men in a disintegrating human order. And not since Epicurus' time has any one appeared, according to our great historian, who discovers the genuine qualities of saviorhood. The enforced, if majestic calm, of Epicurus in his day, and the sublime detachment of a Buddha in an earlier day, are more than reflections of the soul's anxiety. Anguish creates as a sedative for the spirit the idealized figure of one who triumphs over it. Such a figure is the immense figure of a recumbent Buddha which may be seen in Bangkok, a glittering statue that expresses conscious, deliberate abstraction from the realities of the human situation at the very time when a "Day of the Lord" is lowering over East Asia and the world.

The Nazarene of nineteen centuries ago was also called "Saviour." And as we, in this our "Time of Troubles," await on the banks of Time's river in anguished longing for a Deliverer, "a single Figure rises from the flood and straightway fills the whole horizon. There is the Saviour; and the pleasure of the Lord shall prosper in His hand; he shall see the travail of his soul and shall be satisfied."[1] But the figure of Jesus as a Saviour is different from that of all other "Saviors." They were the idealization of human longing; He had different marks from any that man had ever thought of as being the marks of saviourhood.

Jesus came, said Paul, *in the fullness of time*. Time had "reached its grain." It was *kairos,* the time that gave all time its meaning. On looking at the time of Jesus' birth within the context of world-history certain striking things of a clearly providential character impress us. A monotheistic faith, a belief in one God, had, after a long religious struggle, become firmly established in Palestine. Rome, under the leadership of the great Augustus, had organized the mightiest empire which the world had known. Those who lived under the august "Pax Romana" could count upon travel facilities to move from land to land, and citizens could count upon Roman justice. Empire wide propaganda thus became a possibility. The Greek language, the most perfect linguistic instrument ever forged for the communication of ideas, became the chief medium of culture. The stage was set for the advent of a world faith.

---

[1] Arnold J. Toynbee.

In the reception given to Jesus while still a babe we can discern features of profound historical meaning. The time had come when the millennial quest to know the ultimate truth found at length the clue to "all the treasures of wisdom and knowledge." With reason did the Eastern magi say, in Auden's words, when they knelt before the Galilean Child in Bethlehem, "O, here and now our endless journey stops." With equal reason did the shepherds from the neighbouring hills exclaim, on doing obeisance at the same spot, "O, here and now our endless journey starts." For this Birth signified that the time had come when the common people of the earth were to have a fresh beginning in history. New light for thought and new power for life had both come.

The national atmosphere of Palestine was saturated in those days with Messianic expectancy, as the Gospels make clear. All classes were on the tip-toe of hope, that the hour was at hand for Israel's Messiah to appear and deliver his people from their bondage. Jesus the growing boy could not be alien or unsympathetic to patriotic sentiment. Milton, in *Paradise Regained*, puts these words of soliloquy into the mouth of the Son of Man, when, following His Baptism, he wandered the Judean wilderness, recalling his boyhood years and the early passion for justice that inspired him.

> Victorious deeds
> Flamed in my heart, heroic acts one while
> To rescue Israel from the Roman yoke;
> Then to subdue and quell, o'er all the earth,
> Brute violence and proud tyrannic power,
> Till truth were freed, and equity restored.[2]

Jesus had to struggle, as we know, with the temptation to become a great political figure and so fulfill the Messianic hopes of Israel. He declined, however, to assume the flaming role of national patriot. But in doing so, he made clear that the role of

---
[2] Book I.

Israel's Messiah could be interpreted in other terms, and that the initiation of his own public ministry was the occasion for great national rejoicing. For the "hour" had indeed come, the "time" was indeed fulfilled, which had been foretold by the ancient prophets and hailed by the contemporary Baptist in his preaching and symbolic rites by the Jordan. History was now being invaded by the forces of a new order, of a new dimension of spiritual reality. Jesus fully recognized and proclaimed that in Him and in His work the Kingdom of God had come. God's power, in a totally new manner and degree, had entered human history. "Today," said Jesus, speaking in the Synagogue of his native town of Nazareth, "the Scripture has been fulfilled in your hearing." "The Spirit of the Lord is upon me," He said, "because He has anointed me to preach good news to the poor. He has sent me to proclaim release to the captives and recovering of sight to the blind, to set at liberty those who are oppressed, to proclaim the acceptable year of the Lord" (Luke 4:18).

Clearly, therefore, it was a time for joy. There was exuberant joy both in the teaching and demeanor of Jesus in the early period of his public ministry. In his own words, it was the time of the "Bridegroom," a honeymoon time, a time of "new wine" that called for "new bottles," a time "to let the bass of heaven's deep organ blow." But just because it was the "fullness of time," and a time for joy, let men, therefore, "repent." Let them have a total change of mind with regard to God and the world and man; let them undergo a complete reorientation of life. Let them "believe the Gospel," opening their whole being to the "Good News" that God had "come to Captive Israel" and that a new aeon in human history was being inaugurated. The old cycles of history were gone, whereby there was "nothing new under the sun." History had now received a Center, and was moving on towards an end.

The Christ whose coming gave history a fresh start and who Himself became history's center, was a wholly *unique* person. Few things have been more impressive in recent New Testament scholarship than the recognition on the part of distinguished Jewish students of the New Testament that Jesus Christ cannot be paralleled in the religious literature of Israel. What they stress, coming to the study of Him with fresh eyes, and after a bitter struggle with their prejudices, is that the really new thing that Jesus brought into Israel's history was Himself. He was the new thing. Love had been known and spoken about before He came, but never a love of the redemptive quality which He described in His parables and illustrated in His life. The new thing was that God should be represented as going in search of lost sheep, and that Jesus Himself should have been the loving friend and seeker "of the lost." Such a person and such teaching introduced into religion a wholly new spirit and atmosphere. It set redemptive initiative and self-giving sacrificial love in the very heart of Deity.

What is still more striking is that Jesus attributed all that He Himself did to the activity of God. He was no "path-finder" who blazed a luminous trail into the heart and secret purposes of Godhead. There is no Jesus cult in the New Testament. The Man Christ Jesus is rather one born "from above," whom God "sends" into history that he might bring into Time the counsels of Eternity.

But if it is true that Jesus was a unique figure, it is equally true that he was a *representative* figure. When Paul in the Ephesian Letter speaks of the Christ as "summing up" all things, he was describing a characteristic which was as true of the "Jesus of History" as it was, and will be, of the Cosmic Christ. Jesus was the representative of Israel. He summed up in Himself and his mission the history and God-given destiny of the Jewish people. He was the true "seed of Abraham," to whose day Abraham had looked forward (John 8:56). He was David's Son as well as David's Lord. And there is in the Synoptic narrative a parallelism between Jesus and Israel which is too close to have been undesigned. Israel came out of Egypt. So did Jesus after Herod's persecution of the children had subsided. Israel was baptized unto God in the Red Sea; Jesus was baptized in the waters of the Jordan. Israel spent forty years in the wilderness where God proved His people; Jesus was forty days in the desert, tempted of Satan. There is not the slightest doubt also that Jesus deliberately identified himself in the latter part of his ministry with the Suffering Servant of Jehovah, who unquestionably represented Israel in the pages of the prophetic writer. He as Israel's Messiah took over and carried forward the vicarious role of his people. Whatever may be thought of this symbolical connection between Israel and Jesus from the viewpoint of Biblical criticism, no one can ignore its significance from the viewpoint of Biblical theology. There are in the Bible most significant unities which for their discovery, and still more for their understanding, need "eyes of faith."

Jesus also *represented humanity*. He was the new man, the true man, the "son of man." He appears in the Gospels as the perfect, the sinless representative of mankind. God and man he loved with perfect love. His life was God-centered in the most absolute sense. He lived to do His Father's will, to be "about His Father's business"; to fulfill His God-given Mission. He translated the love of God into the most passionate love for men. He "went about doing good." He alone of all the sons of men was able to express in perfect and natural unison the divine righteousness and the divine mercy. The eye that blazed with indignation when the Temple was debased and its holy precincts turned into a hucksters' market, was the same that wept in the presence of a family's grief and at the sight of a doomed city. The flame and the tear had the same source. The hand that grasped the lash to rid the Temple's Courts of unjust merchandizing was the same that caressed children, healed the sick and fed the hungry. The Man Christ Jesus knew also the meaning of violent temptation. The Tempter tried him where every strong man is weakest, at the point of the use of power. But Jesus refused to use power for merely selfish ends, even to keep himself alive; or by a grand publicity stunt to force recognition by his people; or to achieve a worthy objective by wrong methods. While Milton, as both parts of his great Epic make abundantly clear, believed that the decisive part of human redemption was accomplished on the Cross, he followed a sound theological instinct in making Jesus' temptation so utterly crucial. It was in resisting the temptation to put self-interest above obedience to God through faith in God's sovereign guidance of His life that Jesus proved to be the perfect man. In everything relating to human behavior the life of Jesus Christ is normative for man. Whenever Christian morality, or even Christian theology, strays far from, and fails to do justice to, the concrete manner and spirit of Jesus' life, both fall into inevitable aberrations.

But the representative man was more than man. The Second Adam was not a mere son, albeit the greatest son, of the first Adam. This man of God was the God-man. Jesus of Nazareth represented God. He did so because he was God manifest in the flesh. He was God Incarnate. In the words of the Fourth Gospel of the Word of God, the eternal personal word, "became flesh." The writer of the Epistle to the Hebrews speaks of Him as a "Son" who reflects the glory of God and bears the very stamp of his nature. Paul, in the Epistle to the Colossians, which he wrote from Rome about the same time that he wrote the Letter to the Ephesians, speaks of Jesus Christ as the "image of the invisible God, the first-born of all creation." He it is in whom all things were created, in heaven and on earth—all things were created through Him and for Him. In one of the other "prison epistles," the great Letter to the Philippians, Paul represents Jesus Christ as "having been in the form of God," but not thinking equality with God a prize to be graspingly retained, He "emptied himself, taking the form of a servant, being born in the likeness of men." This too is the Christ of the Ephesian Letter in terms of which we shall consider more specifically His redemptive work and victory. This Christ represented God not as one who so opened His human life to the divine in-filling that Deity, finding in His humanity a perfect instrument, became manifest in Him and worked through Him. What we have rather in the Man Christ Jesus is real incarnation, the self-giving, self-emptying of God-head into a man, to constitute thought's greatest paradox and life's redemptive hope.

> How could the Eternal do a temporal act—
> The Infinite become a finite fact?

That, of course, is the problem. But the fact of the God-man remains; the fruits of faith that He was the Son of God also remain.

There is in the Gospel story one portrait of Christ before His death which might be regarded as the essential image of the nature of Him who summed up in Himself all that was most distinctive of Israel, of manhood and of Deity. It is the portrait of Jesus already alluded to who, in a moment of intense awareness as to His identity and His mission, "knowing that He had come from God and went to God," pours water into a basin and washes His disciples' feet. The figure of the Master become the Servant of his servants, of the Highest doing the most menial deed, is the perfect unveiling of the "Mystery of Christ." A young Oxford tutor in philosophy, a professed agnostic in matters of religion, was strolling aimlessly one day down the famous Oxford street called Broad. His eye lighted casually on a display of wares in a bookseller's window. Among the books was a picture, a nineteenth century print of Jesus washing the disciples' feet. As the young philosopher gazed at that portrait something happened. "I knew," he said afterwards to a friend, "that the Absolute was my footman." The inmost nature of Deity as self-giving love, the reality of God become man for man's salvation, was made plain to him. He grasped the "essential image" that what is most ultimate, and the only thing that has a future, in God's great scheme of things, is love that gives itself for others. He saw the foundation truth of God's Order.

The sequel of the foot-washing and the goal of the lowliness that inspired it was the Cross. Water and a towel portray the victory of the God-Man in life; a Cross was His triumph in death.

c) THROUGH CRUCIFIXION CONQUEST

Speaking to his ecumenical audience of the work of Jesus Christ in achieving redemption, Paul presented the sacrificial love of Christ as a pattern for Christians to follow. Said he: "Walk in love, *as Christ loved us and gave Himself for us a fragrant offering and sacrifice to God*" (Eph. 5:2). For Paul, as for the New Testament writers as a whole, the Death of Jesus Christ was crucial to the fulfillment of His redemptive mission.

There are diverse ways in which the Crucifixion may be regarded. It may be regarded as the merest contingency of history. Jowett, a famous Oxford professor of the nineteenth century, used to say boastingly that the only part of of the Apostles' Creed which he believed was the part which reads he "suffered under Pontius Pilate, was crucified, dead and buried." Such an outlook upon the death of Christ regards it as a historically isolated event. At most it stands out as a judicial murder committed by the representatives of an Empire whose pride was Roman justice. In such a case the Crucifixion was simply a miscarriage of justice which illustrated man's inability to achieve his own ideals of justice.

The Crucified Christ has appeared to others as the supreme victim of fate. In Buenos Aires, that leading center of Hispanic culture, whose citizens in the tragic days of the last war had the reputation of being the best fed and best dressed people in the world, there is current a most revealing, if tragic, phrase. When a man of the great metropolis by the River Plate wants to say of some one that he amounts to nothing, that he is a down and out, a pitiful example of sub-humanity, a poor beggar or a poor devil, he says, he is a "poor Christ." He means by this that the human derelict of whom he is thinking resembles the traditional Spanish representation of Jesus Christ, an utterly dead and forlorn Figure. He is thinking of the image of the Crucified whose classical expression is the "recumbent Christ of Palencia," whom Unamuno described as "Death's Eternity," the "immortalization of Death." What we have here is a rather extreme example of religious pessimism regarding the effective redemptive virtue of the Crucified. There exists in secular circles today a disdainful rejection by "men of taste," and by "red-blooded men" in general, of any connection between Christ's Crucifixion and the solution of the basic problems of mankind.

But for Paul the Cross had both historical and cosmic significance. In an event which, for the casual observer, was but a brutal judicial murder, and for men of the world the symbol of sentimental irrelevance, Paul saw the imprint of eternity. An event happened upon Golgotha which was neither historically causal, nor spiritually irrelevant, but which constituted a mighty victory. That event happened once for all for history and the cosmos: never could it be, nor needed it to be, repeated.

This event Paul thought of under the form of a victory. The Crucified was a Conqueror who, in the language of the Colossian Epistle, "nailed" to the Cross the legal charges or "ordinances" against those for whom He died, and "on the Cross" triumphed over "the Principalities and Powers," disarming them and making of them a "public example" (Col. 2:15). To be true to Paul's thought and to the New Testament the Cross of Jesus Christ must be regarded as a victorious assault rather than as a passive victimization. It is only when to the classical and true picture of Christ as the "Lamb brought to the slaughter," we add the equally classical and true picture of the Warrior King "come from Edom with dyed garments from Bozrah and travelling in the greatness of his might," and of a Lamb whose garments are dipped in His own blood, that we get an adequate conception of the doctrine of the Cross, of what, in theological language, is called the Atonement. And, after all, in New Testament Apocalypse the Lamb "slain before the foundation of the world" appears as an essentially active, potent, militant figure.

What does the Atonement mean? Jesus Christ, says Paul, in words already quoted from the Ephesian Letter, "loved us and gave Himself for us" (5:2). Confining ourselves to this letter alone we find a wealth of expressions which Paul uses to set forth the significance of the death of Christ. It is "through His blood" that "redemption" comes to us, and that we receive the "forgiveness of our trespasses." (1:7). It is "in the blood of Christ" that men are "brought near" to God and to one another (2:13). "In the blood of Christ" also Jews and Gentiles were made one; for the Crucified became "our peace" through "breaking down the middle wall of hostility" (2:14). In the Second Epistle to the Corinthians there is a passage which supplements these references to the connection between peace and unity; and which throws light upon the profound inner meaning of the great event. "God," says the Apostle, "was in Christ, reconciling the world unto Himself" (2 Cor. 5:19). That is to say, God was active in the Cross. Viewed in its ultimate significance the death of Jesus Christ was the supreme manifestation of divine, reconciling love. In a word, the Atonement, the event whereby sins were forgiven and forgotten, and whereby the forgiven, reconciled to God and to one another, became "sons of God," was an act of God Himself.

When we realize that the death of Jesus for the sins of the world was an act of God to reconcile the world unto Himself, new light breaks upon the substitutionary idea of the Atonement which is basic in Paul's thinking, as it is in the thought and imagery of the Bible as a whole. It was God who gave Himself in Christ for the sins of the world; it was God who became the Reconciler. In Jesus Christ, the God-Man, God Himself was present in divine fullness. The redemptive action of Jesus was the redemptive action of God. Because God was completely in the Crucified, the separation between God and Jesus, while possible for thought, did not exist in reality.

Light is thrown upon the significance of "blood," of the "blood of Christ" in the Atonement. What does blood mean in Biblical thought? It means the "life." Blood which is poured out, as was the "blood of Christ," is life that is given in anguish and suffering. But there could be no greater error than to limit the correlation of the "blood of Christ" to the physical fluid that oozed from his wounds. In some circles the word "blood" has taken on virtually magical significance. No preaching is regarded as evangelical which does not speak constantly of the "blood." The mere mention of the "blood" becomes a hallmark of orthodoxy and the frequent occasion for a display of orgiastic emotion. But in the deepest sense what was the blood that was shed? The physical blood which was lost by our Lord in his suffering and death, was but a symbol of real blood, of life poured out in anguish, during his whole public ministry. For, speaking in all reverence, the God-Man had to qualify to be worthy of the final act of dying. In the language of the Epistle to the Hebrews, he "learned obedience by the things which he suffered." It was "through sufferings" that he was made perfect. He had to be made meet for death, else the shedding of mere physical blood, which millions had shed in equally painful circumstances, would have been in vain. But from the Temptation onwards to the Cross blood was literally drained from the soul of Christ. The anguish that He suffered, and which He endured so buoyantly and willingly, was also part of the "price of blood." To understand the Atonement let us remember that the Crucified Christ who summed up in himself both God and man, summed up also in the supreme hours of his Sacrifice all that he had suffered for sin and from sin from the time that he stepped out of Jordan till the time he said, "It is finished."

The recognition of the Atonement as an act of God avoids also the very shallow view of the significance of Christ's death which reduces it to the expression of a natural law. Some, by making an illicit distinction between God and the Son of God, regard Jesus Christ as an innocent third party who was made to suffer for the guilty. Apart from the fact that there is no general law in nature or in human life whereby the innocent suffers vicariously for the guilty, and of which this view of the Atonement could be regarded as an illustration, something more serious must be said. The view which regards Christ, the Son of God, as a mere innocent third party behind whose merits guilty men could hide, reflects a tendency to break up the divine Family into a Tritheism and to cast an aspersion upon God the Father. The Son becomes a Hero, but men are repelled by the Father. This false formulation of the Atonement is overcome, however, when we realize that it was God Himself who made the Atonement, substituting Himself for man. Then there is no question of an innocent third party behind whom the guilty can hide. Jesus Christ was innocent, but He was no mere third party. He was God manifest in the flesh, fulfilling all the costly obligations of redeeming man from his sin by meeting in the form of sinful man all the consequences of sin. In the Cross of Christ, therefore, guilty sinners are forced out of every sheltering nook and cranny and brought face to face with God Himself, who in Jesus Christ gave Himself in love for the sins of the world that He might reconcile the world unto Himself. What place is there now for the pursuit of a false godlikeness, for the craving to be like God, without God, and to rival God? The broken, forgiven sinner can only say to the Saviour who loved him and gave himself for him:

> Thou, O Christ, art all I want,
> More than all in Thee I find.

Not yet, however, have we considered concretely the specific modes in which Jesus Christ achieved a redemptive victory. Having emphasized the truth that what was involved when Christ "gave Himself for us," dying "for our sins," in what we call the Atonement, was an act of God, it is now necessary to consider the forces which He had to overcome before He could be called in the fullest sense the "Saviour." We cannot hope to solve, it is true, the mystery of redemption. We cannot formulate an adequate human theory to express so divine and infinite a fact. But it helps thought, and attempts a reasoned account of fact, if we try to grasp the concrete situation which the Saviour of mankind had to face in his redemptive work, and in which he overcame.

Jesus' first great encounter as the Redeemer of men was with *Law*. The God-Man who represented the sinful human race, and set himself to constitute a new humanity, had to take due account of the moral order established by God, under which all human life had to be carried on. In the hierarchical moral order it was laid down that the lower should render to the higher loving obedience and to one another mutual love; and that the higher should show towards the lower loving concern. This order, which had its source in God's Nature of which it was the expression, bound the spiritual universe together. Of Jesus Christ it can be said, as we follow the course of his life from childhood to the Cross, and upon the Cross, that He was loyal to this moral order. He was lovingly obedient to God His Father and was lovingly concerned about all who were in need. In the most absolute sense he loved God and His fellow-men, and so fulfilled the Law.

And this He did, let it be observed, not because He strove to do so, but because it was His nature to do so. That is to say, Christ's devotion to the Law of God was not a legalistic pursuit of love, but a spontaneous movement of love. There is a paradox of moralism as there is a paradox of hedonism. He who pursues happiness as his goal never becomes happy. So, too, he who pursues goodness as his goal never becomes good. The most he can become is a Pharisaical prig; though what he will likely become is a despairing neurotic. The truly good person is one who does the good without thinking of goodness or the rewards of goodness, out of pure love to God and his fellow-men. But in this sense Jesus Christ was the only *good* person who ever lived. He was so because in Him Love came. He was Himself Love's purest essence. In Him Love was not a garment which He put on in order to play a part; it was a perennial fountain within Him which inspired all His actions. We can say, therefore, of Jesus Christ that He fulfilled perfectly the divine moral order. He qualified to be the pioneer and the first fruits of a new humanity.

More difficult was Jesus' encounter with the concrete will of God for His own life. For obedience to the Moral Order means not only general obedience but very specific obedience to God's commands for personal behavior. And this, too, Jesus did, accepting all the painful implications of his Messianic mission. With filial obedience He accepted and drained to its dregs that "cup" which the Father gave Him to drink. In simple faith in God, and in loyal obedience to God, He plunged into the last dark defiles of His redemptive path. And there, in the most hidden and enigmatical phase of His redemptive task, He met, on man's behalf and as his representative, the consequences and sanctions of a violated moral order, the reality of God's justice. As the Sinless One who took the place of sinners and pioneered the way for the manifestation of new sons of God, He came to know in the bitterness of His soul and in a way that we can never understand that the "wages of sin is death." He suffered and He triumphed.

This leads us to the second encounter of Jesus Christ, His encounter with *Sin*. Sin, as we have already seen, is in its essence, the affirmation of self-will over against God's will. Sin means the attempt by a finite spirit to become God's rival. When the inner logic of sin works itself out evil becomes good.

Throughout His whole life, but especially between the time when water was poured upon Him in the Jordan, till blood poured from Him on the Cross, the Son of God engaged in grim contest with sin. The demonic powers assailed Him and strove to divert Him from His chosen way. We simply cannot understand the life of Christ, or do justice to the great drama of redemption, unless we take seriously the supernatural powers of evil who figure in the background of all Biblical thought and who carry on an organized strategy. But the Tempter was frustrated. After the wilderness effort he "left Jesus for a season." Our Lord after He had heard of manifestations of power which His disciples had wrought in His Name "saw Satan fall from heaven." "The Prince of the world cometh," he said on another occasion, and "findeth nothing in me."

> Ill wast thou shrouded then,
> O patient Son of God, yet only stood'st
> Unshaken! Nor yet stay'd the terror there;
> Infernal ghosts and hellish furies round
> Environ'd thee; some howl'd, some yell'd, some shriek'd,
> Some bent at thee their fiery darts, while thou
> Sat'st unappall'd in calm and sinless peace! [3]

Sin in human beings vented itself upon the Redeemer. There was the fickleness of the multitudes whom He so assiduously taught and so tenderly cared for and who at the last cried "Crucify Him!" There was the religious fanaticism of the spiritual leaders of Israel who broke the spirit of the Law in their attempt to define the letter. There was the lack of spiritual perception on the part of His disciples which tried frequently to turn Him from His course. Among the chosen band, and beyond all mere absence of insight, loomed up Peter's disloyalty and Judas' treason. Yet to no sinful word or attitude did Jesus ever succumb.

Sin encastled in institutional forms where vested interests had their seat was particularly ruthless. For expediency's sake the Jewish hierarchy, to defend their interests, repudiated the "Just" One. Also for the sake of expediency, a Roman Governor, to ingratiate himself with a rebellious race and prove himself "Caesar's friend," condemned to be crucified a man in whom he had found no fault. But Jesus, withal, did not allow Himself to become embittered. He continued to show the most loving concern for men. He loved also His enemies. Sin in every form did its worst against Him. But ere He breathed His last He said, "Father, forgive them, for they know not what they do."

And so Jesus died. He died in grim encounter with Death, the

---
[3] *Paradise Regained*, Book IV, lines 419–425.

last Enemy, after all the other enemies had been vanquished. He died upon a tree and so became a literally accursed thing, according to the religious tradition of His people. Sin could do no more; the Law could exact no more; men could expect no more. Darkness came down on Golgotha. It was now for God to speak. Was what had happened an unusually brutal judicial murder, but still a mere contingency of history? Was it an event spiritually irrelevant to the problem of history and of the human heart?

Says the Ephesian Letter, speaking for the New Testament, Jesus Christ "gave himself for us." (5:2). He "brought us near," Jews and Gentiles, to God and to one another "by the blood of His Cross," bringing to an end thereby the "enmity," the bitter age-long hostility (2:14). How do we know? God "raised him from the dead and made him sit at his own right hand in the heavenly places" (1:20). The everlasting gates were lifted up; the "King of Glory" entered in.

Before Jesus died Death was man's chief terror. It spelt frustration for human hopes; it was the sombre gateway to a realm of shadowy existence replete with dread and bereft of vital meaning. But by His death Christ saved Death. He "made Death our mother," to use the phrase of Miguel de Unamuno.[4] In her dread womb He engendered a new race of men. He made her the medium of rebirth and the organ for promoting great spiritual ends. He evangelized Death. To be "crucified with Christ," to "be dead with Christ," became henceforth the prelude to new life; to die for Christ became the goal of many an ardent dream. How and why the change? Jesus Christ became the Crucified Conqueror of Death: "God raised him from the dead" (1:20).

d) EXALTATION

"The third day he rose again from the dead; He ascended into Heaven and sitteth on the right hand of God the Father Almighty." So runs the great affirmation in the Apostles' Creed,

---

[4] In *The Christ of Velázquez.*

echoing the Ephesian Letter and the historic faith of the Christian Church.

Calmly, uncontroversially, unapologetically Paul states the fact of Christ's victory over death by His resurrection from the dead. It is in striking harmony with the rhapsodic liturgical character of the Epistle to the Ephesians that the proclamation of the Resurrection is made in connection with a prayer (1:15–23) that the ecumenical Christians to whom he wrote should obtain insight into the practical significance for their lives that God raised Jesus from the dead. He prays that the God of our Lord Jesus Christ, "the Father of Glory" might give them such insight into Jesus Christ that they would become fully aware, first, of the hope that was implicit in their Christian calling, second of the wealth of glory involved in belonging to Jesus Christ, and, third, of the vastness of the divine power which was operating in them and which was available for them. The measure of this power is the resurrection of Christ. "I remember you in my prayers," he says, "that you may know what is the immeasurable greatness of his power in us who believe according to the working of his great might which he accomplished in Christ when he raised him from the dead and made him sit at his right hand in the heavenly places, far above all rule and authority and power and dominion and above every name that is named, not only in this age but also in that which is to come" (1:16–21). Just as Paul, when referring to God's Election does not present the doctrine as a cold theological dogma, but to explain to Christians what it was that had happened to them and the transcending significance of their Christian profession, so, too, in this instance. He wants them to know the possible range of experience and of activity that may be theirs, because the same power that God used to raise Christ from the dead is available for them. Because Christ Risen is theirs and because they are "in Him," infinite power is at work in them, and can work through them. They who were chosen in Christ "before the foundation of the world" shall work and triumph in Christ who has been exalted above all worlds. The highest wisdom, therefore, is to know experimentally this highest power.

Had it not been for the Resurrection all that Jesus Christ was and said and did in His life and in His death would have been futile and in vain. His memory would most likely have been forgotten. Or it might linger on as a glistening, phosphorescent sheen on the ocean tides of history. It might have become the source of many a tragic testimony in prose and verse and in the plastic arts that all is vanity, and that the universe is uninterested in true heroic worth. But by the Resurrection Jesus Christ was vindicated. All the promises and purposes of God that had centered in Him reached their fruition. A new cosmic era had begun; a new order of reality had come to the birth. History would now move on towards its end, with all its forces subject to Jesus Christ, who would also be its Judge at the last. The Christian, the spiritual order created by Him and owing its allegiance to Him, would outlive history.

What took place when Christ rose from the dead is, like his Incarnation and Atonement, a mystery. What is clear, however, is that in a body, the same and yet different from the body of His flesh, because endued with new qualities, He returned to life, and that "ascending to the Father" He became the cosmic Lord of history and the Divine Head of the Church. One cannot think of the centrality given to the Resurrection in the New Testament without realizing that what lies before Christians when this life is over is no mere shadowy, ghostly bliss. The real goal of God's purpose for man will be fulfilled not in the hour of his death, but when he too is raised from the dead, a spiritual body, and plays his part in the larger purposes of God when the historical drama has come to an end.

But the hidden things of tomorrow can be left with God. For us Eternity is now, so far as the great issues are concerned. Paul's purpose in the Ephesian Letter was not to indulge in an apocalyptic reverie, making display of his knowledge of things that "eye hath not seen nor ear heard," nor yet to satisfy the natural curiosity of his readers then and now to know concerning things to come. His own purpose was to fix in his readers' minds this tremendous fact, as the basis of their faith and work in this world, namely that, "Jesus Christ is Lord." The Saviour who united them to God and to one another, who became their peace and the source of their light and strength, was the Sovereign Lord, the Ruler of the Universe and the Head of His Body the Church.

Let us like them, in obedience to Paul's desire, ponder for a moment what the Sovereign Lordship of Jesus Christ means.

God "has put all things under His feet" (Eph. 1:22). The course of history and the spiritual destiny of the universe are both in the hands of Jesus Christ. There can be no failure or frustration. The Ruler of history is no "young fighting Deity," of limited resources and uncertain future, to use H. G. Wells' fanciful concept. Jesus Christ shall reign till every foe of God's purpose is vanquished. How His triumph will be achieved, whether by a special personal manifestation of His glory to inaugurate His spiritual reign, or by a special outpouring of His Spirit upon the Church as the historical instrument of His will, is not the important thing. The important thing is that the Risen Christ is no detached spectator of the events of human history; and the future is with Him.

God has made Jesus Christ "the Head over all things for the Church which is His Body, the fullness of Him who fills all in all" (1:22, 23). The chief concern of Jesus Christ is the Christian Church, which is His Body. It is not civilization or culture or the political order. His concern is that His Body shall be what God's purpose has designed it to be. When the Church is the Church, when, in its empirical reality and historical existence it truly functions as the Church, it will prove to be in history the instrument of God's glory. When civilization, culture, and the political order are prepared to recognize the Church and to take seriously what the Church stands for, then the secular order will gain in purity, unity, and stability. A true secular order depends upon the Church, but the Church does not depend upon a sympathetic secular order.

Not being a Kingdom of this world, the Christian Church owes its allegiance to Jesus Christ alone. No human hierarchy has the right to usurp Christ's authority in the Church; no secular state has the right to make the Church the instrument of its policy; the Church dare serve no other master but Christ. In this revolutionary time, when the state in different forms has had the pretention to enserf the Church, and make it the servile agent of its will, one great declaration of the Church's faith and mission stands out above all others. It was formulated in the German city of Barmen in the time of the Nazi tyranny. "We reject the false doctrine," said the signers, "that there are spheres of life in which we belong, not to Jesus Christ but to other masters; realms where we do not need to be justified or sanctified by Him."

Proclaiming in the Pauline spirit, as set forth in the Ephesian Letter, "the unsearchable riches of Christ" (3:8), making "all men see what is the fellowship of the Mystery which was hid in God who created all things by Jesus Christ" (3:9) the Christian Church, will partially in this world, and completely in the world to come, be the "fullness of Him who fills all in all" (1:23).

We must now enquire what it is that Paul tells us concretely concerning the new type of manhood and womanhood which Jesus Christ creates, the community which he calls the Church, how it originates, who its members are, and in what manner they should live.

CHAPTER V

New Men in Christ

God's purpose in history and in the cosmos involves two things. It involves, as we have already seen, the establishment of a new center of spiritual relationships in which "things in heaven and things in earth" are brought together. That center God constituted in Jesus Christ. Jesus Christ, in virtue of what He was in Himself as the God-Man, and by the life which He lived among men, by His death on the Cross for human sin, by His glorious resurrection and His ascension to "God's right hand," became the center of a new order of reality. That new order, which was revealed to St. Paul, who regarded himself as its "steward" or "executor," is the "mystery," God's open secret, which is proclaimed to mankind in the Gospel.

The purpose of God involves, however, something else. It involves the establishment of a relationship between men and Jesus Christ, this new center of spiritual unity. By becoming united to Christ men are lifted out of their self-centeredness; their hostility towards God and towards one another ceases; reconciliation takes place in Jesus Christ, their "peace." From being "children of wrath," members of a community alienated from God, they become "sons of God," members of a new community called the Church. This means a total adjustment of their lives towards God and his purposes. The pursuit of a false god-likeness, the desire to have God's attributes without submitting to God's authority, comes to an end. Men who are reconciled to God become His adopted sons and seek to do His works.

a) "IN CHRIST"

This new spiritual relationship is characterized by St. Paul as being "in Christ." Students of Pauline thought as different from one another as Adolf Deissmann and Albert Schweitzer are agreed that the phrase "in Christ" is the central category of Paul's thinking. This phrase "in Christ," or "in Christ Jesus," is used by Paul in his letters, according to Deissmann's calculation, some one hundred and sixty-nine times. What does Paul mean by this vital category? The distinction must first be made between "in Christ" and "in the heavenlies." By the latter phrase Paul means more than a spiritual condition; he means the supernatural sphere. But this sphere is also the seat of spiritually hostile powers. To be "in Christ" is therefore more than to be "in the heavenlies"; it is to have one's status in the very life of God and to draw one's sustenance from God in Christ; but one is not thereby in any mystic sense beyond all conflict. The readjustment of life to God in Christ, to live "in the heavenlies in Christ Jesus," means to live henceforth a God-centered existence, living by God and for God, amid all the realities of spiritual conflict. In a word, to be "in Christ" does not mean to be beyond struggle; it is not absorption into a state of transcendental calm.

To be "in Christ," let it be further observed, is wider than to be "in the Church." It is through a relationship to Christ that a man becomes related to the Church which is "His Body." But Christ is greater than the Church. The Church is the reality where His fullness, the "pleroma," appears; but the Church does not exhaust Christ nor bind nor limit Him. When God's vast cosmic plan comes to full realization there shall be found "in Christ Jesus," among "all things in heaven and in earth," a structure greater than can be formed by merely human spirits. For that reason Paul carefully distinguishes between Christ and the Church. He says in a great doxology in the Ephesian Letter, "To Him [God] be glory in the Church and in Christ Jesus" (3:21). A human spirit is related to the Church because he is "in Christ."

There would appear also to be a real distinction in Paul's thinking between "in Christ" and "in the Lord." The phrase "in Christ" denotes the transcendental relationship to Christ. Christians, for example, were "created in Christ Jesus for good works" (2:10). In concrete living, however, they act "in the Lord" (6:1). They are to be "strong in the Lord" (6:10). The "Lord" is the standard and director of all true Christian living. It is the distinction between Christ as the cosmic spiritual Reality who is above all worlds, and the concrete living Presence who is found on all the roads of earth.

What is important to realize is this. To be "in Christ" implies spiritual renewal, a "new creation." It is quite meaningless to speak of anyone being "in Christ" who has not been "made alive" (I Cor. 15:22). Those who were "destined to be God's sons through Jesus Christ" (Eph. 1:5) were made alive together with Christ (I Cor. 15:22) and raised up with Him and made to sit with Him in the heavenly places in Christ Jesus (Eph. 2:6). Such people will, from henceforth, organize and determine all their attitudes and actions from their new center, Jesus Christ. They will exercise discernment and discrimination. They are the people, who, according to Paul, form the Church. That being so, and this is important for all our thinking from this point onwards, the Church in this ultimate sense, a fellowship of men and women "in Christ," has no meaning whatever for St. Paul save as a living fellowship with one another because they have fellowship with Christ.

b) MEN IN CHRIST

Whatever else may be in doubt regarding the full significance of Paul's favorite expression "in Christ," of this there is no doubt. To be "in Christ" means total spiritual change. Those who are "in Christ" have been given not only a new status and are related to a new source of strength; it is theirs to allow themselves to be possessed by Christ, to strive to conform their lives to Christ, to endeavor to "learn" Christ, to "know" Christ (Eph. 4:20). Their passion is or should be to become one with God's purpose in Christ. In this total spiritual renewal are included all those facets of inner change which are commonly spoken of as regeneration, conversion, repentance. However diverse the actual types of spiritual experience may be, depending as they do upon the background of the individual involved and the particular operation, as we shall see later, of God's "grace," men in Christ are people in whom a new principle of life has been implanted, the direction of whose life is different from the mass of mankind and whose outlook has been reoriented towards God. They sum up in themselves the triple reality of being regenerate, converted and repentant. When they are true to their new status and relationship, Christ is their life as He was for Paul. He becomes the soil in which they grow, the atmosphere which they breathe, the source and goal of their entire existence as men. The man who wrote the Ephesian Letter spoke of himself as a "man of Christ" (II Cor. 12:2) and said, "To me to live is Christ," that is, "Life means Christ to me" (Phil. 1:21).

Such men are "persons" in the Christian and only true sense of the term. They have responded to God. They are true men because they have come to know and to submit themselves to the Man and to God's purposes in Him. Because of their relationship to Jesus Christ, the image of God, that god-likeness which was the essence of their human nature reappears in actual existence. Their manhood is restored in Christ. When they cease trying to be God and instead submit themselves to God, their humanity, that is, their true human nature, is reborn. The true movement, therefore, is from essence to existence and not from existence to essence.

Those who, like the Frenchman Sartre, affirm that man has no essence, that the only thing you can say about him is that he exists, say so because they deny that there is a God. It is true, of course, as Dostoevski said, that "if God didn't exist anything would be possible." The human task would then consist in man's quest of an essence, of a true nature. But man had an essence which became corrupt; in Christ that pure, undefiled essence has been restored. Men "in Christ" rediscover themselves when they discover Him. Their human essence becomes manifest in Christ-like existence. A much greater thinker than Sartre, the Spaniard Unamuno, diagnosed the atheist's real trouble to be the realization that, were he to admit God's existence, he would have to be a very different type of personality from what he knew himself to be. In a famous sonnet Unamuno puts on the atheist's naïve and candid lips these words:

"If thou shouldst exist, then I also would really exist." [1] The perennial human problem is man's refusal, through pride or fear, to accept God's gift of true existence, which is offered to him "in Christ."

There is nothing comparable to the experience of "really existing," to that rapture of the soul which comes when one realizes the meaning of being "in Christ." When manhood is restored in Christ, the Christian soul becomes more than a mere type. He who awakens to what it means to be "in Christ" becomes an "individual" in an intenser form than ever before. For it is the glory of God, as he is revealed in the Bible and in Jesus Christ, that He individualizes. To adapt a line of old William Blake, God does not save and label men by the barrel-load. In one of the Psalms

---

[1] "Si tu existieras existiría yo también de veras."

(87:4–6) God is represented as inscribing in his census role the names of individual Egyptians and Babylonians, thereby regarding them as native born sons of Zion. Men who are "in Christ" have more than a group consciousness. The full significance of being "in Christ," of being "sons of God," does not break upon people unless they come to the awareness of the personal love of God towards them as individuals. There is nothing more elemental in the Christian religion, nothing that can develop more fully the meaning of being "sons of God," of being "in Christ Jesus," than the awareness of a personal debt of gratitude to Jesus Christ and of a personal relationship to Him. While it is true that such an overmastering sense of belonging to Christ can produce Christian individualism and make collective action and a churchly sense oftentimes difficult to achieve, it is equally true that there can be no substitute for "souls," for strong, loving individuals who know whose they are and whom they serve and who can give a reason for "the hope that is in them."

One is surprised, in this connection, to discover how a contemporary writer on the Epistle to the Ephesians can make a statement of this kind: "Many attempts have been made to expound what Paul meant by 'in Christ.'" He says, "We must beware of those who speak of a mystical personal union with Christ. There is little of the individual pietism of either the mystic or of Evangelicalism in Paul. For he was a Jew and the Jews thought in corporate terms." [2] Now this completely ignores the fact that in the Psalms, that greatest repository of religious devotion, a devout writer can address himself directly to God and say, "Thou art *my* God," and that Paul, the Jew who had the most complete sense of the corporate, churchly aspect of Christianity that ever mortal had, wrote not only, "Christ loved the Church and gave himself for it" (Eph. 5:25), but also, "Who loved *me* and gave himself for *me*" (Gal. 2:20). In response to that in-

---

[2] F. C. Synge, *St. Paul's Epistle to the Ephesians*, p. 2.

dividualizing love of Christ, Paul of Tarsus had throughout his life—call it mystical, call it pietism, call it what you will—a passionate sense of personal relationship to Jesus Christ. F. W. H. Myers is absolutely true to the New Testament record when, in his *St. Paul*, he makes the man who "saw," "heard," was "crucified" with Christ, "lives" in Christ, say,

"Christ! I am Christ's! and let the name suffice you."

The plain truth is that an exclusive emphasis, or an overemphasis, upon the corporate or churchly meaning of being "in Christ" tends to destroy the most basic and priceless thing in the Christian heritage. This is precisely what has happened in the Roman Catholic tradition, especially in Hispanic countries. The sense of living fellowship with the Risen Lord progressively disappears and is discouraged. The Church, which has become Christ's patron instead of his servant, provides for the faithful, in a multiplicity of Virgins and Saints, all sorts of objects for their ardent devotion. The Lord Himself is kept under very strict surveillance. Can it be wondered at that this fear, this literal horror, of Christian individualism, should be, according to the contemporary evidence, the best possible preparation for Communism? When the Christian soul is schooled in losing himself in a religious mass, in a vast ecclesiastical corporation, it is not hard for him, when he loses his religion, to become lost in a secular mass, in a vast political collectivism. And this is happening at a time when, according to well-informed students of Russian Communism, a sense of the importance of the personal and individual begins to reassert itself.[3] There is nothing that can meet the bane of anonymity in our time, whether in the secular or in the religious order, but a resurgence of evangelical Christianity, a rediscovery by lonely human atoms what it meant to be "men in Christ."

---

[3] Sir John Maynard, *Russia in Flux*, p. 492.

c) BY GRACE

But how do men come to be "in Christ"? How is Christian personality born? How are men "saved," delivered from self-centeredness to Christ-centeredness? The answer of Paul in the Ephesian Letter to this question is, "By Grace" (2:8), by the Grace of God. By *"grace"* Paul means, the active, compassionate, redeeming love of God. It is the activity of his love, his unmerited favor, his *agape* which "destined" men to be "his sons," which provided Jesus Christ the Redeemer (1:6), and which lovingly and potently influenced the lives of men in order that they might believe upon Christ and receive the forgiveness of their trespasses (1:7).

Paul's emphasis upon the Grace of God brings us face to face with the fact that we have to do with no passive ideal order but with active love. Human beings are not called upon to aspire after a spiritual realm of perfect forms and satisfactions. Men are not asked to lift themselves, by a supreme act of will, out of their mundane grovelling and to soar aloft, as on eagles' wings, into "heavenly places" where God dwells and is ready to receive them. No, God comes to the soul now, as He came to the world in Jesus Christ. He loves men passionately in all their wayward and unlovely moods. His love follows them, encompasses them, in all the dark recesses of their lostness and alienation. For the great minds of Greece the pity which such an attitude presupposed was a disease. Deity surely could not be less unruffled and unperturbable than ideal men. Hinduism has never been able to relate the love of God to the love of men. Love in Buddhism promotes an abstention from harming but it does not engender a passion for healing. But so far as the God and Father of Jesus Christ is concerned, it can be said, "Where sin abounded grace did much more abound" (Rom. 5:20).

But how does God come to the soul? In what manner does His Grace operate? Sometimes it booms like "the bursting of the

Sea." Sometimes it thunders like "the battering rams of Boanerges" that pounded at Ear Gate in Mansoul.[4] Sometimes it leads a man to say with Bunyan's Pilgrim, "I was driven out of my native country by a dreadful sound that was in my ears; to wit, that unavoidable destruction did attend me, if I abode in that place where I was."[5] It came to Paul in a Voice that pulled him up in his anti-Christian fervor, "Saul, Saul, why persecutest thou me" (Acts 9:4)?

At other times God's Grace manifests itself less dramatically, but none the less effectively. It comes to the soul "like a still small voice." It comes like "the drift of pinions," the filmy feathers of a bird's wing against "clay shuttered doors." Or it comes in sorrow, which turns out to be the shadow of God's hand "outstretched caressingly."[6]

As to the manner in which Grace operates, all depends upon the human situation, the state of the soul. But in every case strength is combined with beauty. And in every instance what God in His Grace wants is a response, a disposition to let him in who stands at the door, to open the casement to the light, to accept the overtures of love, to submit to the imperious voice which says, "Follow me." But whatever the approach, provided the response is real, life's rhythm from that time on is "to the praise of His glorious grace" (Eph. 1:6).

For God's Grace does not operate merely once in the life of the person who submits to it. The principle of *sola gratia* ("grace alone") continues through the whole of life. Christians live by the Grace of God. In their weakness, when human strength has ebbed away, and appearances are all against the Christian soul, the same voice sounds, that timeless, timely Voice, "My grace is sufficient for thee" (II Cor. 12:9). With reason Paul was accustomed to conclude his letters, as the Bible itself also concludes,

---

[4] John Bunyan, *The Holy War*.   [5] *The Pilgrim's Progress*.
[6] Francis Thompson, *The Hound of Heaven*.

with the words, "The grace of the Lord Jesus Christ be with you all," or "with all the saints."

d) THROUGH FAITH

But how, from the human point of view, does God's Grace become really effective in life? What is the nature of the response that makes man's life the sphere of God's action? For God never violates human personality. He never intrudes himself where he is not wanted. He took risks with man in his original creation by giving him freedom of choice; he continues to respect the free choice of man to accept or to reject His Grace. Man's positive response to God's Grace is Faith. "By Grace have you been saved," says Paul, "through Faith" (Eph. 2:8).

Faith is openness towards God. It is the decision to accept what God gives, to allow God to work *in* one as he has worked *for* one. It is opening one's whole being to the incoming of God as the Saviour of life; it is the total response of the human spirit to the command of God as the Lord of Life. It is in the fullest sense an attitude of trust in God. Christian faith is very much more than what has been called the "Protestant principle," that is, a certain critical sense of beyondness, a reaching out into the unknown, a dissatisfaction with everything hitherto achieved. Christian faith is rather a very definite, trustful, adventurous commitment to God Himself, who through the open gateway of faith brings into the soul all that is meant in the Bible by His "Kingdom," His "Righteousness," His "Light," His "Knowledge," His "Glory." Through Faith God's new era breaks; through Faith His new order comes. Faith is thus reception which gives new perception. It is the recognition of the fact that we come to know God when we have become known by God; for the God we come to know is the God who comes to us. He comes to us in His grace that we may go to Him with our faith.

If this is, in general terms, what faith is, then it must be clearly distinguished from other interpretations of the way in which contact is established between God and man. Diverse views have been propounded as to how, in an ultimate sense, truth can be attained, how the human self can achieve ideal selfhood, how the welfare of mankind can be accomplished. All of these views are ways in which, in some sense or another, the initiative originates with man, so that the outcome becomes man's achievement.

The first way is the *way of knowledge*. This might be called the Greek way. It is based upon the conviction that what man most needs in order to fulfill the human ideal is correct information, clear thinking, inspired by the love of truth. This view underlies the modern cultural development. It presupposes two things that are not borne out by experience, first, that man, by searching, can know ultimate truth; second, that man, when his own self-interests are concerned, is a disinterested seeker of truth. But even though man were to achieve perfect knowledge, wisdom, in the most absolute sense, his wisdom could not, as Pascal pointed out, produce a single sentiment of love. And, without love, no real human problem can be solved. Without love, moreover, God cannot be known.

There is, in Christian circles, a form of the way of knowledge which merits a brief passing reference. Theological orthodoxy, that is, right thinking about God, is a noble and necessary ideal of the Christian religion. But, unfortunately, right ideas about God can become a substitute for a right relationship to God. Men subscribe to ideas, they protest their loyalty to ideas, they challenge others to show where their ideas are wrong. But they forget that it is quite possible to have the most orthodox and unchallengeable ideas about God, about the Incarnation, the Death and the Resurrection of our Lord Jesus Christ, and be no more than pure pagans so far as a personal relationship to God the Father and Jesus Christ his Son is concerned. They have scholastic knowledge but they lack evangelical faith. And, for that reason, they suffer from the defect, which, according to Paul, is inseparable from those who have knowledge without love: they become "puffed up" (I Cor. 13:4), proud, censorious, arid, even cruel, a terrible witness to the fact that it is possible to know about Christ without knowing Him. And what of those who pride themselves on being authorities on everything relating to the road that leads to the "Celestial City," who yet themselves have never trodden that road as pilgrims? Some there are, too, who presume to have that kind of secretarial relationship to Deity which gives them authoritative knowledge of the apocalyptic blueprint of all the coming ages, who nevertheless have never learned to live and serve God in the time that now is.

Another way is the *way of virtue*. This is the old Jewish way. It is the way of those who have a passion for goodness, who strive to live in accordance with Law, with the highest ethical ideals. But, apart from the fact that no one can achieve perfect goodness both in the spirit and form of his action, those who try to do so become either soulless Pharisees or unhinged neurotics. It is as true today as it always was, "By the works of the Law shall no flesh be justified" (Gal. 2:16). Man does not reach true manhood nor do God's will by making some ethical precept his Deity. The attempt to live in an absolute sense by legalistic prescriptions, so far from its attaining ethical perfection, wrecks moral personality and human relations. Much of the world's evil is due to "good" people who insist on applying principles which are inapplicable, or who force men to obey laws which they are incapable of observing.

There is also a way which might be designated *the way of bargaining*. It was the way of the old Canaanitish religion. Its inspiring principle has been stated by students of religion in the Latin words "Do ut des." "I give in order that Thou mayst give." The worshippers of Baal bargained with their divinity. They gave that they might receive in return. *Do ut des* religion has marked popular Catholicism in Latin American countries. The status and treatment given to images of the Saints in the homes of simple people have depended upon the way in which they fulfill sacred bargains. What else but a "way of bargaining," *Do ut des* relations with Deity, can we call the whole system of indulgences in the Roman Catholic Church? When promises are made to worshippers that in return for certain sums of money corresponding spiritual privileges or satisfactions can be secured, we witness in religious relations a Christian reversion to pagan primitivism. The inculcation of the idea that religious rewards involving the favor of Deity can be purchased with money is a total denial of the Christian meaning of faith and an utter degradation of the Christian emphasis in religion.

Two other spiritual absolutes might be mentioned which have in recent times been popular competitors of Christian faith. One might be called the *way of ancestry*, the other the *way of association*. Rosenberg's *Myth of the Twentieth Century*, which proclaimed that the Nordic race was the Messianic race, the race of destiny, illustrates the way of ancestry. The simple fact of being a German gave one the same ultimate status in relation to the Deity that an ancient Jew possessed because he was a child of Abraham. The moment membership in a race or nation is given absolute worth, another ground of universal goodness is proclaimed. But over against all such presumption regarding the ultimate worth of nation or race, the word sounds in the New Testament, "God hath declared all under sin" (Gal. 3:22). "There is none righteous, no, not one" (Rom. 3:10). "The just shall live by faith" (Gal. 3:11). It makes no difference to God from what racial stock a man has stemmed.

The *way of association* grounds ultimate standing and worth upon the group to which one belongs. Marxism does this in the glorification of the revolutionary proletariat. How difficult to convince a Marxist that "all have sinned and come short of the glory of God" (Rom. 3:23), and not merely the capitalists? The "righteousness which is of faith" (Rom. 9:30) means nothing to a Marxist because "the radiant forces of the Universe" are automatically on the side of the disinherited masses.

What is particularly painful to think about, however, is that there should exist a doctrine of the Christian Church so grossly mechanical as to maintain that merely to belong to the institution called the Church and to be loyal to it guarantees one's ultimate standing with God. We cannot escape the fact that the Roman doctrine of the Church whereby, upon the basis of unquestioning loyalty to the institution, a man's standing with God is absolutely guaranteed, is a very crude form of salvation by association. In its practical results, this doctrine is an obstacle to the development of mature Christian personality. In principle it is a violation of the nuclear truth of New Testament Christianity that it is by faith, personal faith in God, and by such faith alone, that a man is justified before God and made a partaker of the Grace of God. And yet the same crude un-evangelical trend can be found in many Protestant churches. How frequently does Church membership, the mere payment of dues and a sufficient number of attendances on religious services to prevent being taken off the Church roll, become the equivalent of salvation by association, and a virtual denial of salvation by faith?

This excursion into other ways to ultimate righteousness, which are human substitutes for faith in God, prepares us to deal more concretely with the meaning of faith. Thus far we have found faith to be an openness towards God, a trust in God. But Christian faith is openness and trust that are inseparably related to Jesus Christ. For Paul, as for New Testament Christianity, "saving" faith is faith in Jesus Christ which makes the soul open and trustful towards God. As Jesus Christ is at the center of God's Grace, that is, God's gracious movement towards man, He is no less at the center of man's apprehension of and response to God's Grace. It is in Christ that God comes to the soul; Christ is God's gift to the soul. It is the soul's discernment of Christ as supremely worthy that awakens faith in response. Thus faith itself is a gift of God because it is the encounter with Jesus Christ and the awareness of his spiritual excellence that gives it birth.

Faith in Jesus Christ is, on the one hand, an *assent* to the truth about Christ, and on the other, *consent* to the reality of Christ. Faith does not take place in a vacuum. It comes by "hearing," as Paul said in his Letter to the Romans. And "hearing" comes by the Word of God. Christ is proclaimed; things about Him are brought to the attention of a man. What the man hears about Christ commends Him as one whose claims are worthy to be believed, and as a Saviour and Lord to whom one ought to commit one's life. To assent to Jesus Christ does not necessarily mean, at faith's beginning, the mind's adhesion to an elaborate theological statement regarding Him. It means rather that He stands before a man as the One who makes a unique, an absolute appeal as the Saviour. Then, not blindly, but with all his faculties functioning, the man gives himself, in unreserved commitment, to Jesus Christ. Out of that commitment will come in due course a unique knowledge of God and an equally unique experience of the power of God. So far as Paul himself was concerned, he said to Jesus Christ at their first encounter, "Lord, what wilt Thou have me to do?" He said later, after he had know Him long, "I am crucified with Christ, nevertheless I live, yet not I but Christ liveth in me, and the life which I now live in the flesh, I live by the *faith of the son of God,* who loved me and gave himself for me" (Gal. 2:20).

Being "crucified with Christ," Paul regarded himself as a dead man and so recognized no past charges against him. Jesus Christ with whose death he was identified had taken care of the whole past record of his sinfulness. "Being crucified with Christ" he recognized no present claims upon him save the claim of Jesus Christ with whom he rose from the dead, who lived in him, and by faith in whom He now carried on his life. Thus faith in Jesus Christ, really to believe on Christ in a Pauline sense, means that Christ has assumed complete control of one's whole being. Evangelical faith is something much richer and more radical than the acceptance of God's forgiveness of our sins for Christ's sake, it involves also the acceptance of Christ's sovereign lordship over our lives. That is to say, to "accept Jesus Christ" means to accept gratefully what He has done *for* us, but also what He wills to do *in* us and *through* us. For the Christian is no longer his own, to do his own will; he belongs henceforth and forever to His Saviour and Lord, Jesus Christ, who died for him and who lives for him. We receive Jesus Christ without cost because of what He has done for us, but it becomes costly business to receive him, because of what He will do in us. God's free grace in Jesus Christ, to which faith responds, becomes costly grace when Christ takes command.

When the true significance of evangelical faith is grasped certain criticisms that have been directed against it fall to the ground. It is said that the doctrine of God's forgiveness upon the basis of what Christ did involves a grave depreciation of justice. It tends also, it has been alleged, to produce a spirit of cynical braggadocio among certain people: what Christ did for them gives their moral worthlessness a new sense of importance and constitutes an invitation to fresh sin that they may receive God's forgiveness. If forgiveness is so free, why not indulge oneself, running up moral debts to the limit, in order to take advantage to the very full of the divine forgiveness?

W. H. Auden interprets this mood of opposition to be the evangelical view of forgiveness. "Justice," he makes one of his characters say, "will be replaced by Pity as the cardinal human virtue, and all fear of retribution will vanish. Every corner boy will congratulate himself: 'I'm such a sinner that God had to come down in person to save me. I must be a devil of a fellow.' Every crook will argue: 'I like committing crimes. God likes forgiving them. Really the world is admirably arranged.' And the ambition of every young cop will be to secure a death-bed repentance." [7]

Two things are here forgotten. It is forgotten that faith's acceptance of the Crucified is accompanied by a deep hate of the sins that led to the Cross. It is also forgotten that Faith's accept-

---

[7] Cf. *A Christmas Oratorio.*

ance of the Risen One commits the forgiven sinner to a new life, and relates him vitally to the Lord of Life.

So important in fact is faith in the life of a Christian that it is not only the means whereby he enters into life, it becomes also the permanent attitude of his life. A Christian not only began to live when faith awoke him. His new-awakened life became a life of faith. "The just by faith shall live," said Paul. They shall go "from faith to faith." As they go, they will move onwards, towards one frontier of life after another. They will not close their eyes to facts. They will not fall into a mood of optimistic self-deception, believing that everything will come out all right in the end. They will rather live by the grace and follow in the steps of the "Pioneer and Perfecter of faith," the Christ who beckons them to a pilgrim, crusading life.

e) UNTO PEACE

But such a life, lived upon the frontiers of thought and action, is conditioned upon the reality of peace. Faith produces peace and peace becomes the condition of a continued exercise of faith. "The Peace of God" becomes the guardian, the garrison of the Christian soul.

The Ephesian Letter throws a luminous shaft of light upon the place and significance of peace in the lives of the new men. Previously they had lived in a state of tension and strife. They had been estranged from God and had been at enmity with one another. "But now in Christ Jesus you who once were far off have been brought near in the blood of Christ. For He is our *peace*, who has made us both [Jew and Gentile] one, and has broken down the dividing wall of hostility . . . that he might create in himself one new man in place of the two, so making *peace*, and might reconcile us both to God in one body through the Cross" (2:13–16, RSV).

Peace, as well as Grace and Faith, is intimately associated with Jesus Christ. "He is our Peace." Two things need to be said about the peace which Christ gives. It is a peace which is based upon reconciliation and it is a peace which is fulfilled in action.

Christian peace is based upon reconciliation. It is primarily peace with God, the peace that comes when estrangement ceases and the soul is brought near to God. It is a vision of the Cross, of the deep significance of the "blood of Christ," that produces this sense of reconciliation between God and man. It instills peace into a spirit which is sad, restless, and apprehensive because of a sense of sin and guilt.

Nowhere in Christian literature is the connection between spiritual peace and a vision of the Cross described so perfectly as in Bunyan's *Pilgrim's Progress*. "Just as Christian came up with the Cross," we read, "his burden loosed from off his shoulders, and fell from off his back. . . . Then was Christian glad and lithesome and said with a merry heart, 'He hath given me rest by his sorrow and life by his death.' Weeping for sheer gladness and with a deep peace in his heart, he gave three leaps for joy, and went on singing

'Blest Cross! blest Sepulchre! blest rather be
The Man that there was put to shame for me!'"

The man who knows the peace that comes from a sense of sins forgiven and of reconciliation to God is predisposed towards reconciliation with those whom he hated before. The old ego full of pride and self-importance, which always finds some occasion to show resentment, has passed through the agony of death into the joy and peace of new life. The new man, unburdened and free, and full of gratitude to God for His unspeakable kindness to himself, becomes an agent of the kindness and peace of God in the lives of others. Paul mentions how, through the Cross, the historic rift, the deep seated hostility between Jew and Gentile, was overcome. Christ reconciled both to God and made them one body in Himself. The peace that reigned among Jewish and Gentile Christians was not based upon a new-born spirit of mutual appreciation which was willing to let bygones be bygones; it was not a newly forged alliance to promote certain common ends. It was rather a peace, a reconciliation, brought about by the fact that the old issues were all dead issues. They were *one* in Christ Jesus; they were members together of *one* body. Here clearly is the pattern for dealing with every kind of human antagonism. Let the foes be brought near to God at the Cross, and there, receiving God's forgiveness and forgiving one another, become one body. Let them henceforth know the "fellowship of the blood of Christ" (I Cor. 10:16). Let the blood, the life, that was given for them, now be communicated to them, and surge through them, as members of one body. It is the will of God that the corporate unity into which formerly antagonistic groups are brought when the "peace of God" reigns in all hearts, should be patterned upon this first and most decisive reconciliation. Among "men in Christ" there is absolutely no place for maintaining the rights and priorities, for perpetrating the prejudices and antipathies that marked former relationships between them as members of different races, nationalities, classes and castes.

Such peace, such harmonious unity, however, can only be maintained in action. Christian peace is not an end in itself; it is a means to an end. It is the indispensable prerequisite for God's will being done by an individual Christian and by a Christian group. The moment peace is sought as life's most desirable goal, it is lost. Abiding peace is like happiness; God gives it only to those who serve Him. It is given only to those who "will one thing," to those who are willing to "know only Jesus Christ and him Crucified" (I Cor. 2:2). "The peace of God which passeth all understanding" is given to pilgrims and crusaders. It is bestowed upon them by the wayside as they rest from their toil in order to equip them for further toil. It is peace on the Road and for the Road.

This peace is pricelessly described in the *Pilgrim's Progress*. Christian has been entertained in a wayside home by Piety,

Prudence, and Charity. "They discussed together till late at night; and after they had committed themselves to their Lord for protection, they betook themselves to rest. *The pilgrim they laid in a large upper room, whose window opened towards the sun-rising: the name of the chamber was Peace; where he slept till break of day.*" In the morning Christian took farewell of his hostesses. Before the day was done he had fought the fiend Apollyon in the Valley of Humiliation in the greatest battle of his career; and most of the night that followed he marched through the horrors of the Valley of the Shadow of Death. But Peace made strong his heart and he knew not the meaning of fear. Christian peace is peace for the Sun-rise, and also for the deep Valley where the light does not shine by day. It is peace for the darkness that comes when the sun goes down; it is peace also for the "morning without clouds" that lies beyond the valley, in the realm where the traveller shall have "rest at the last."

It is but natural that Christian peace should be so if it is really the "Peace of Christ." When Jesus Christ said to his disciples, "My peace I leave with you, my peace I give unto you" (John 14:27), it was the night before he died. He was intensely aware of what lay before Him, but His soul was at peace. That peace He bequeathed to His disciples as His most precious legacy. The peace which Jesus Christ gives to His followers is peace for action, peace for the Road, peace to do the will of God. It is not the peace of grave-yards where quiet beauty reigns in the midst of death. It is rather the peace of the river on its way from the uplands to the sea. The river is at peace because its bed is made. Whether its waters shoot the rapids, or swirl through sunless caverns, or mirror sunlight on their way across some placid meadow, the river is at peace. It is at peace because, beyond the mountains and the plains, the ships and the mills, is the ocean, and the "rest that remaineth."

f) FOR "GOOD WORKS" IN THE CHURCH'S SERVICE

The men whom God "makes alive," who have become "men in Christ," are "destined" by God to a life of active goodness. The supreme manifestation of their spiritual status, and of the fact that Grace, Faith, and Peace are actively operative in their lives, is found in their "good works," in the practical fruits that they bear. One never ceases to be impressed with the emphasis which the New Testament places upon behavior as the *sine qua non* of true religion, and the ultimate criterion by which it will be judged by God and should be judged by man. No amount of knowledge, however true, no amount of talk about true Christianity and of violent denunciation of false Christianity, can ever be a substitute for "works of love."

There is in the *Pilgrim's Progress* of John Bunyan—to quote once again this classic of the Christian life—a priceless, and, as I have found it, a sobering description, of a man called Talkative, who was in his own esteem a Christian paragon. When invited by Faithful to state his views on the outward evidence that a man was a true Christian, one who knew the grace of God in truth, Talkative gave these two marks: first, "a great outcry against sin," and second, "great knowledge of Gospel mysteries." With withering scorn and Biblical proof, Faithful rejects both criteria. It is one thing, he says, to cry out against sin in others and quite another to abhor it in oneself. And, as for knowledge of divine truth, "A man," says Faithful, "may know like an angel and yet be no Christian."

It is no less true that "men in Christ" must live for more than the expression of emotion, whether religious feeling seeks its supreme outlet in liturgical pageantry or in orgiastic outbursts. In the Christian religion knowledge and feeling have a noble and important place, but neither should be cultivated for its own sake; nor is either an infallible proof of true godliness. Christians do not become "sons of God" by their works, but it is by their works alone that they prove themselves to be "sons of God."

The "good works" to which "men in Christ" are called manifest themselves primarily within, and on behalf of, the Christian community, the Church. The circle of fellow Christians is the sphere where "good works" must primarily become operative. For the community of the redeemed has an importance and an ultimacy which belongs to no other social group. God, says Paul, made Christ "the head over all things for the Church, which is his body" (Eph. 1:22, 23). Speaking for himself Paul regarded it to be his highest and most creative endeavor to suffer for the Church's sake, "to fill up what is behind of the afflictions of Christ, for his Body's sake, which is the Church" (Col. 1:24). Leaving until next chapter all discussion regarding the ultimate nature and historical reality of the Church, let us, at the close of the present chapter, draw attention to the fact that "men in Christ," by belonging to Christ belong also to a community of kindred spirits in this world. This is true whatever particular view of the Church Christians may hold. We become related to Christ singly, but we cannot live in Christ solitarily. Our introduction to Him may have been an intensely individual, self-conscious thing, as if spiritual reality were limited to a meeting between an infinite Thou and a sinful, human I. But Christ immediately introduced us to kindred spirits who were also "in Him." Paul went for a period into the solitary wilds of Arabia, but he eventually came back to Damascus and went up to Jerusalem to confer with those who had been "in Christ" before him.

The Christian community is inescapable. It is both the ultimate instrument of God's purpose and the immediate sphere for Christian action. Paul prayed that his far-flung constituency of readers should come to know the grandeur and significance of "God's inheritance in the Saints" (Eph. 1:18). It was only when they came "with all the Saints" that they could "have power to comprehend" the true dimension of the knowledge-surpassing "love of Christ" (3:18, 19). For that community was really a "dwelling-place of God" in the Spirit (2:22). No wonder therefore that the chief sphere of the Christian's action should be with and for other Christians, members with him of the Body of Christ. How perfectly Paul's emphasis on the social nature of Christianity agrees with the words of Jesus Himself, "Where two or three are met together in my name, there am I in the midst of them" (Matt. 18:20)!

It is impossible, therefore, to be a "man in Christ" in good and regular standing and be an absolute individualist. The importance of the Church and the interests of the Church must ever be a primary concern of every Christian. He cannot be a Christian in the fullest sense except as a member of the Christian community; he cannot fulfill his mission as a Christian and as a man unless the Church has a large place in his thinking and he finds in it an appropriate sphere for his action. The admission, of course, must be made that there are Christians who, for one reason or another, have never found a spiritual home in any organized Christian community. This was the case with the great Spanish Christian, Miguel de Unamuno. Such Christians are not uncommon in the Hispanic world. There are "men in Christ" who are not inscribed members on the roll of any church. It is much more common, however, for people to have good and regular standing in the Church as a visible society without being "men in Christ." Such people are in the Church, but the Church is not in them. They have never come to see the Church's true greatness nor has the Church a supreme place in their devotion. As church members they do not live in unreserved surrender to the Church's Lord.

Such a person, in the early part of his ministry, was Thomas Chalmers; a man, who, in the judgment of his fellow-countryman, Carlyle, was the greatest Scotsman since John Knox. Chalmers was religious by nature. When it became his turn, as a student of divinity, to conduct worship in the college chapel, his public prayers were so eloquent that the townspeople of St.

Andrews would turn out to hear him lead devotions. He was also a brilliant mathematician. Political economy, a science still in its infancy, was another of his favorite studies. Early in his ministry he aspired to the Chair of Mathematics in the University of Edinburgh which had fallen vacant. Professor Playfair, the retiring professor, had made a public statement to the effect that the Governors of the University should not consider for the Chair any minister of the Church of Scotland. No churchman eminent enough could be found for the high distinction. Chalmers was wounded to the quick at the mathematician's reflection upon the Scottish ministry. He wrote and published an anonymous pamphlet in which he maintained that no group in Scottish society was in a more favored position to devote itself to the Liberal Arts than the clergy. Those were the days of religious "Moderatism." To be a good fellow, to be a member of a literary coterie, to be decent and well-balanced, were higher qualifications for the ministry than to have evangelical fervor. What Chalmers wrote told more of what he and a multitude of other ministers at that time thought of the Christian Church and the ministerial office than it did of their proficiency in the humanities. Here are some of his irate sentiments:

> The author of this pamphlet can assert, from what to him is the highest of all authority, the authority of his own experience, that after the satisfactory discharge of his parish duties, a minister may enjoy five days in the week of uninterrupted leisure, for the prosecution of any science in which his taste may dispose him to engage. In as far then as the command of time is concerned, it will be difficult to find a situation in the country more favourable to the free and uninterrupted exercise of the understanding. . . . A minister has five days in a week for his own free and independent exertions; and it would be a most ridiculous display of argument to prove that there is any thing in the employment of the remaining two calculated to extinguish his mathematical ardour, to stupify and degrade his faculties, to shut his mind against the fascinating enjoyments of science, or to destroy any of those vigorous and

decided tendencies which nature or habit may have implanted. There is almost no consumption of intellectual effort in the peculiar employment of a minister. The great doctrines of revelation, tho' sublime, are simple. They require no labour of the midnight oil to understand them,—no parade of artificial language to impress them upon the hearts of the people. A minister's duty is the duty of the heart. It is his to impress the simple and home-bred lessons of humanity and justice, and the exercises of a sober and enlightened piety. It is his to enlighten the sick-bed of age and of infirmity; to rejoice in the administrations of comfort; to maintain a friendly intercourse with his people, and to secure their affections by what no art, and no hypocrisy can accomplish—the smile of a benevolent countenance, the frank and open air of an undissembled honesty. . . . The usefulness of such a character as this, requires no fatiguing exercise of the understanding to support it; no ambitious display of learning or of eloquence; no flight of mysticism; no elaborate discussion; no jargon of system or of controversy.[8]

In the thought of Thomas Chalmers at that time the ministry was a leisured profession. There was nothing in the service of the Christian Church to claim all the time, all the devotion, all the intellectual vigor which a man possessed.

The years passed. The young Scottish minister underwent a profound religious experience. In a word he became converted. "Christ," "Grace," "Faith," "Peace," "Works," the "Church" took on new meaning for the "new man in Christ." Christ and the Church now had all there was of him. His evangelical passion enhanced and transfigured his great intellectual powers. Mathematics, astronomy, political economy, philosophy and a matchless eloquence, all of them were laid upon God's altar for Christ and His Church. It was Chalmers' lot to live his life in one of the most critical and creative periods in Scottish Church history. The State had attempted to deprive the Church of spiritual freedom, insisting that local patrons should have the right to

---

[8] "Observations on A Passage in Mr. Playfair's Letter to the Lord Provost of Edinburgh relative to the Mathematical Pretensions of the Scottish Clergy" (Cupar-Fife, Printed and Sold by R. Tullis, 1805).

appoint incumbents to Scottish parishes. Chalmers led the great "Disruption" in 1843 whereby five hundred ministers relinquished their churches and manses and faced penury rather than submit to the imposition of the secular power.

On a certain occasion, years after the publication of the famous pamphlet just referred to, the question came up in the Scottish General Assembly as to whether a parish minister should be allowed to hold another whole-time position in addition to his pastorate. The proponent of the motion looked knowingly at Chalmers, who was present. The latter arose, and there ensued one of the most dramatic and memorable moments in the history of ecclesiastical debate in Scotland. After detailing the reasons which had led him to write the famous pamphlet in defense of the abilities of the Scottish clergy and their right to use five days of the week for any pursuit which interested them, he concluded with these words: "Strangely blinded that I was! What, sir, is the object of mathematical science? Magnitude and the proportions of magnitude. But then, sir, I had forgotten *two magnitudes*. I thought not of the littleness of time—I recklessly thought not of the greatness of eternity."

This is the issue, the question of proportion and magnitude. I have referred to the case of Chalmers in order to set in high relief the inherent importance of the Church and the service of the Church for all "men in Christ." Not all should be its full-time ministers, in a professional sense, but all should be its devoted sons and daughters. The great Mother will provide them with the inspiration and strength needed for their secular calling. Their secular calling will provide them with resources which the Church needs to fulfill its mission.

CHAPTER VI

The New Divine Order

Life is a vale of soul-making and souls are more important than civilizations. But souls are not made in solitude nor were they designed by God to live in solitariness.

In the United Commonwealth of Earth and Heaven envisioned in the Epistle to the Ephesians, and which it is God's purpose to establish, souls, and not nations or races, institutions or classes, will be the ultimate units. But when in Christ the cosmic breach has been restored, and the rift in God's creation has been healed, the individual sons and daughters of the Almighty, united to God and to one another, will be members of a vast structure, a cosmic community, a new Divine Order. That Order, established in Jesus Christ, its Creator and Center, is now in process of formation. Within its scope will be embraced all that Paul includes in "all things in heaven and in earth," more than redeemed human spirits, more than the Church which is Christ's Body. He means to convey by that impressive phrase a resultant cosmic order formed by created spirits and founded in Christ, in which God shall be all and in all. The integrating center and also the pattern of that Order will be Christ and the Church.

a) THE "CHURCH WHICH IS HIS BODY"

Without allowing our imagination to riot in futile speculation regarding the eventual form of God's order, two things are apparent. The community called the Church, which occupies a central place in the Ephesian Letter, is presented by Paul in this document, as in other writings of his, under two aspects. There is the Transcendental Community and the Historical Community. Both together form the "Church which is His Body."

The Transcendental Community

By the transcendental community, more commonly called the Church Invisible, is meant the complete number of God's elect, the society of the redeemed, those who have, through Christ, been reconciled to God. This community is made up of the "saints" who have finished their earthly course, and of the "faithful in Christ Jesus" who militate on earth, and whose certain identity is known to God alone. Its members are "men in Christ." They only, in the deepest and most ultimate sense, belong to the Body of Christ, which shall not be completed or perfected as a corporate unity until the close of history, when God's purpose shall have reached fulfillment.

The members of the Body of Christ become related to Him who is their Head as individual units. They are His "new creation," His "workmanship." He "brought them near." As their "Peace" He reconciled them to God; He made them "one new man," "One Body" in Himself. And Christ Himself, the victorious Head of the Church, God made to be "Head over all things for the Church." The fortunes and perfecting of the Church will thus constitute the true finality of history, which is under the sovereign sway of Jesus Christ, the Church's Head and history's Lord.

This community, the Body of Christ, which is both the "fullness of Christ" and the sphere in which Christ Himself reaches His fullness, is from another point of view, "God's inheritance in the saints" (Eph. 1:18). Moses had said, "The Lord's portion is his people; Israel is the lot of His inheritance" (Deut. 32:9). The Church is God's "portion," God's inheritance. Paul prayed that his readers might become aware of what God was getting out of his investment in Christ, what his "inheritance" would really amount to before His divine concern for "men in Christ" came to an end. Elsewhere Paul had said, "Eye hath not seen nor ear heard, neither hath it entered into the heart of man, what God hath prepared for them that love Him" (I Cor. 2:9). We have already noted that at the last the study of the Church is to provide angels with their greatest object lesson into the "many-colored wisdom of God." And no wonder! For, apart from the victory of Christ and God's dealings with the Church throughout history, and all the fascination of that epic, "angels and archangels and all the host of heaven" would contemplate, in the completed community of Jesus Christ, "all the glory and honor of the nations." They would, in a word, gaze upon a world redeemed. In the Transcendental Community would be found a "world." In the community of the redeemed would be every representative human type and every noblest gift and talent, renewed by Christ. The new humanity would greatly outshine the first Adam and his children. The words of Tennyson may be interpreted in a much more significant way than the poet, with his optimistic evolutionary philosophy, had intended.

> Till the peoples all are one and all their voices blend in chorus
> "Hallelujah to the Maker; 'It is finished,' man is made."

But this community began on earth; much of it is still on earth. As the "great Mother," the "Jerusalem which is above," it becomes the archetype for the historical community which militates on earth.

The Historical Community

As the victory of Jesus Christ was accomplished in history and all "men in Christ," become related to their Saviour and Lord in history, the Church which is Christ's Body exists within history as much as it exists above and beyond history. It is a historical community as well as a transcendental community. Its members have lived from the beginning in closest relationship to all the forces and conditions that determine the life of mankind in time and in space.

Certain affirmations can be made regarding the Church as an historical community. Let us now make these affirmations before passing on to consider certain questions suggested by the Ephesian Letter regarding the nature, the constitution, and the policy of the Church in history.

1. The Christian Church is *the Church of Jesus Christ*. Those Christians, men and women who confessed Jesus as "the Christ, the son of the living God," of whom and to whom Paul wrote, who were the historical "first fruits" in the non-Jewish world (Rom. 16:5) formed themselves from the beginning into communities called Churches, "ecclesiae." Those who belonged as members to the "ecclesiae" in Jerusalem, Antioch, Rome or Corinth were people "called out" of the general community; they were "saints" or people "set apart" who came together for the worship of God through Jesus Christ and lived for the service of Christ. Such people, the "faithful in Christ Jesus" (Eph. 1:1), constituted in Paul's thought the "new Israel." Each local *ecclesia* was not an isolated unit, for in each was the reality of the One Church of Jesus Christ. The several *ecclesiae* were communal determinations of that transcendental spiritual reality; the "Church which is His Body." It is important to bear in mind that in the thought of St. Paul, as in the New Testament as a whole, the Church has two meanings, and two only: the Church Universal, in heaven and on earth, which is the *new man*, the One

Body, the Body of Christ; and local organized Christian communities called *ecclesiae*. The Church as an historical community gets its churchly reality from the union of both these: the living presence of Jesus Christ the Head of the Church, and the association of Christians in the name of Christ. The Church in this sense is the true bearer and meaning of history, because it is in and through the Church that God's eternal purpose in Jesus Christ is unfolded. It shall therefore outlive all historical change.

2. The Church, when it is truly the Church in the pristine, New Testament meaning of the term, is *composed of people who have been "made alive,"* who have passed through a radical death and rebirth, who constitute a "new Creation." Its members have been "sealed with the Holy Spirit" (1:13), the manifestation of whose gracious working in their lives is the token or guarantee that eventually they shall be completely sanctified from sin and become perfectly godlike in their nature. It is clear, therefore, that any kind of human association whose members are not bound together by a common faith in Christ and a common experience of renewal by Christ, cannot with any propriety be called a Church.

3. Those who profess this common faith and share in the common experience, are related to one another in *congregations*. As the individual is the ultimate unit of the Church Universal, the Body of Christ, so the congregation is the ultimate unit of the historical community called the Church. But congregation in this sense need not be limited to a local community; it may embrace those "gathered together" from many local communities who profess the same faith and share in the same experience and who desire to render corporate obedience to Jesus Christ and the Gospel. The moment Christians desire to render corporate witness to Christ in a wider than local context, and arrange to come together in Christ's name to consider questions relative to His cause in the world, they constitute, by their action in so doing, an historical or empirical expression of the one Body. This will involve, as

indeed it has involved historically, that some Christians who become servants of the Church in this wider expression of its reality must find their personal Christian fellowship within the wider "congregation," rather than be limited to the association provided by a local Christian community. This needs to be said; otherwise it would be impossible to speak with any propriety whatever of the Church as an historical community. There would be communities, but no community.

It is nevertheless true, as Karl Barth has recently emphasized, that the pattern of the Church must ever be the group of people met together in one place who are gathered together by the "Word and Spirit of the living Lord Jesus Christ." What constituted the Church, says Barth, is the "event" or "gathering of his people together by the living Lord." [1] The congregation is the event which consists in gathering together (*congregatio*) those men and women (*fideles*) whom the living Lord Jesus Christ chooses and calls to be witnesses to the victory which He has already won, and heralds of its future universal manifestation. Thus the Church is the living congregation of the living Lord Jesus Christ "which needs to be constantly recreated by Him." The local congregation is naturally the "primary, normal, visible form of the event" because of the fact that the meeting takes place in a parish or district with clearly defined boundaries.

By speaking of the synodical congregation, Barth does not limit churchly reality to the local Christian community or ecclesia. This reminder, however, is basic and salutary, and in accordance with Pauline and New Testament thought, that what makes a Church is the united response to the call of the living Lord Himself. No association of Christians is constituted a "Church" once and for all. It may become no more than "dead appearance," an association no longer in touch with living spiritual reality, but concerned

---

[1] "The Church—the Living Congregation of the Living Lord Jesus Christ" in *Man's Disorder and God's Design* (Harper & Brothers, New York).

only with "museum pieces," a monument to the memory of God instead of a witness to His glory. But when the living Lord is present in power in His "congregation," whatever be its physical bounds or numerical dimension, you have in truth a Holy Community. You have a fellowship rather than an institution. You have people whose primary concern is to be in harmony with Jesus Christ. The ultimate criterion to distinguish a false or moribund Church from a true and living Church is the presence in power of Jesus Christ Himself.

4. The Church as an historical community *has been* and *continues to be, greatly divided*. We have the three great Christian traditions, Roman Catholicism, Eastern Orthodoxy, and Protestantism. The first of these traditions has centered churchly reality in the institutional order, the second in mystical fellowship, the third in the Word of the Gospel. There are besides in our time a very great diversity of denominations within the Protestant tradition. Some of these have been the fruit of religious schism, but many owe their origin and separate existence to racial, linguistic, and cultural circumstances. But at this present time it would appear that the centrifugal movement which has marked the history of the Christian Church for many centuries is now giving place to a potent centripetal movement towards unity.

5. The Christian Community in our time seeks in different ways and by diverse means to *give concrete, historical form to the unity which is real in the one Body of the transcendental Church*. Following a period when the Kingdom of God and the promotion of a diffused spiritual influence derived from Christ took the place of an effort to commit men to Christ as members of a fellowship of faith, a new sense of the Church has been born. The emergence of new Churches in different parts of the world as a result of the Christian missionary movement; the spirit of unity created by world-wide missions; the fact that in the recent persecution of the Christian religion by totalitarian powers it was only churchmen and Churches which withstood to the death

and refused to submit: all this has given rise to a new sense of the reality and importance of the Church.

Coincidentally with a reborn sense of the Church, and the movement towards Christian unity known as the Ecumenical Movement, there has manifested itself in Christian circles everywhere a new desire to relate Christianity to life. The laity, that is, those who are not the paid full-time servants of organized Churches, display a quickened sense of Christian responsibility to "copy God" and to "learn Christ"; they are moved to "baptize into Christ" their secular vocations. The Churches, individually and corporately, feel their responsibility to challenge the whole secular order, society and its institutions and the state itself, in the name of Jesus Christ. The new awareness of the fact that Jesus Christ is not only the Head of the Church but also the Lord of history, leads the Christian Church to make clear to citizens and rulers in the secular order that obedience to the laws of God is the only foundation of public purity and order, and that righteousness, right relations between God and man and between man and man, constitute the only basis for international understanding. The vision of an Order of God over against the Disorder of man is growing, and the historical community, the Church, is being moved by the Spirit of God to accept and fulfill its historic role.

In order to understand more fully the nature of the Church of Jesus Christ as a community in history, and receive guidance to solve its problems and shape its destiny in this our time, let us, in what remains of this chapter, listen to the wisdom and the spirit of the great first century architect of the Christian Church who wrote the Ephesian Letter.

b) IMAGES OF THE CHURCH

It will help us to grasp the historical reality and role of the Church if we begin by examining the three images, or pictorial representations of the Church, which are used by Paul in his

Epistle to the Ephesians. While these images were designed by him to describe different facets of the Transcendental Church, they are of first rate importance in considering the Historical Church. The Church in history will fulfill its true mission in the measure in which it too aspires to be, and succeeds in being, the *Building*, the *Bride*, and the *Body* of Jesus Christ. These great images are the patterns or archetypes of what the Church is and should become. As we consider each one in turn let us remember that they are figures, images, metaphors. Each enshrines one or more facets of essential Christian truth. But they must not be studied allegorically, as if every single detail in the figure were significant. That is to say, these figures are parables and not allegories.

1. *The Building*

The first figure used by Paul to set forth the meaning of the Church is that of a building, a sacred edifice, a temple. This figure, drawn from the material realm, presents the Church as a structure of which God is the Builder and which He Himself indwells. As a building the Christian Church belongs to history. It represents the concrete communal continuity of God's purpose throughout the ages. The prophets of the Old Covenant and the Apostles of the New Covenant are associated together in its foundations. The Corner Stone, the immense foundational slab which gave unity and stability to ancient structures, is Jesus Christ. The stones, the living stones, of which the temple is composed, are believers in Christ. They are people who made the great Confession which Peter made, and which constitutes the basic affirmation or loyalty upon which the Christian Church is founded. Peter's Confession, "Thou art the Christ, the Son of the living God"—that, and not Peter himself, became the historical foundation of the Christian ecclesia. By making that confession the first Christians indicated that they had heard, understood, and responded to the call of Jesus Christ. They became thereby living stones in His Church, which He said would outlive all historical change, defying the very "gates of Hell," every attempt of Satanic power to frustrate God's purpose in Him. The fact that Peter himself, and not his Confession, has been made the foundation of the Christian Church by a great Christian Communion represents the greatest single calamity in the history of the Christian religion. The position of the Roman Church in this respect violates the clear meaning of the words of Jesus Christ. It does an immense injustice to impulsive and devoted, but in crucial moments, fickle and myopic, Peter. It runs counter to the New Testament as a whole and to the genius of the Christian religion. It has no place in the sublime imagery of the Church as a building of which "Jesus Christ Himself is the chief corner stone" (Eph. 2:20).

The rock-like stability and age-long security of the Christian Church, is not designed, however, to make Christians complacent and give them a sense of false security. New living stones must continue to be added to the incompleted building, and those there already, and those still to be laid in the sacred structure, must "grow into an holy temple in the Lord." Christ's followers, members of His Church, must, by the quality of their discipleship in adhering closely to their Lord, contribute to the unity, strength and completeness of the Church. What is required of all the separate blocks is a collective adjustment to the Corner Stone. It is obvious that to make his idea plain, Paul strains the figure of the building. There is no doubt in the least, however, that what he agonizes to convey is the idea that the Church as a temple is soundly constructed, not merely by the addition of fresh blocks but by their progressive unified relationship to the "chief corner stone." He implies that structural unity and strength are more important in the Church of Jesus Christ than mathematical accretion and bulk.

While Paul, in his eagerness to drive home the great ideal and prerequisite of unity "in the Lord," does not here refer to other significant aspects of the symbolic temple, he would surely want his readers to reflect upon this fact that a "holy temple" is not like any ordinary structure. Without the Presence the temple has no meaning, it is not what it was designed to be. The Christian Church, when it is truly the Church, is the Home of the Presence. Under the New Covenant as under the Old, God not only calls His people and makes them into a chosen community; He also abides, tabernacles with them. "The Lord is in His holy temple." At the risk of mixing metaphors, let us remind ourselves, that, according to New Testament thought, the "Corner Stone," the living Lord Jesus Christ, is also the "Glory in the Midst" of His Church. Paul had said of individual Christians, "your bodies are the temples of the Holy Ghost." He said also in the Ephesian Letter, "Grieve not the Holy Spirit of God" (4:30). Each individual Christian, and still more, the Christian Church as a whole is a cathedral. But only in the measure in which the tabernacling Presence is "in the midst," is a Christian soul or a Christian Church a witness to God's glory. When the Presence is fled neither soul nor Church is anything more than a monument to God's memory.

2. *The Bride*

Paul also used the figure of a bride to denote the status of the Christian Church in relation to Christ. As the figure of a temple emphasizes historical stability and permanency, that of a bride emphasizes the apocalyptical hope of the Church, its ultimate triumph at history's close. The Church is Christ's Betrothed who during her earthly existence should maintain herself loyal and pure against the celestial nuptials. In his second letter to the Corinthians (11:2) Paul thinks of a given local congregation as a bride of Christ. He had striven, he says, to present the Corinthian *ecclesia* as a "chaste virgin to Christ." In the Ephesian Letter, after making the relationship between Christ and the Church the basis and pattern for the marriage relationship among Christians, Paul breaks out into this rhapsodical passage: "Husbands," he says, "love your wives, as Christ loved the Church and gave Himself up for her that He might consecrate her, having cleansed her by the washing of water with the Word, that the Church might be presented before Him in splendor, without spot or wrinkle or any such thing, that she might be holy and without blemish" (5:25–27, RSV).

This sublime passage is one of the great sources of Christian mysticism. The relationship between God and His people, which Hosea describes in plaintive and moving language as that of a husband passionately devoted to an unfaithful wife, passes in the New Testament into the relationship of Christ and His Church. Only by tender, passionate devotion to the Beloved, only by the constant aspiration after perfect holiness and Christlikeness, can the Christian Church, individually and collectively, respond worthily to the sacrificial love and ceaseless concern of Jesus Christ. Deathless loyalty and spiritual purity are the great desiderata. The great Christian concern becomes, Would this word, this action be worthy of Jesus Christ? While it is true that it is the Church collectively, and not the individual Christian soul that is the Bride of Christ, it is both pardonable and legitimate that individual Christians should have felt the allurement of this great figure to express their personal love for the Redeemer. For if bodies can be "temples," souls can be "brides"; and those passionate lovers of the Bridegroom, Teresa of Ávila and Rutherford of Anworth, will continue to speak to and for the deepest soul of the Christian Church. A constant danger of sentimentality there, of course, is; and Christians and the Church must ever be on their guard against it. But in contemporary Protestantism there is no present danger of sentimentality in the expression of devotion to Jesus Christ. Neither is there any great evidence of a resurgence of the mystic fervor which distinguished the Church's greatest days. In Roman Catholicism, on the other hand, the crude promotion of the Virgin Cult has sapped the root of Christ Mysticism in that Communion.

3. The Body

The third, the greatest, and the most characteristic figure which Paul uses in the Ephesian Letter to describe the Christian Church is that of a body. The Church is the Body of Christ. Sometimes, in Paul's thought, Christ is the Head of the Body; sometimes, He is the whole Body, of which Christians are members. It is in dealing with this celestial image that we must be particularly careful not to allegorize the details.

Chosen from the most familiar biological realm the Body expresses function, instrumentality, mobility. As such it is the figure for which the road, service, conflict have special meaning. Never can a body fulfill its function if corporal cultivation becomes an end in itself, if physical exercise and the pursuit of health serve nothing beyond themselves. A body is truly a body when it is the servant of thought and spirit. A body achieves the true glory of the corporal when it gives itself up, and even loses physical life for that which is more than body.

As in the figures of the Building and the Bride, adhesion to Christ is the great thought which Paul desires to convey. This thought can be expressed much more naturally and adequately by the Body than by the Building. For as the principle of life and movement is native to the body, progressive, structural adhesion to Christ characterize the individual members and the body as a whole. They all strive together to achieve harmony with the Head. The question as to the goal of bodily activity is, therefore, of paramount importance.

The goal of the Christian Church as the Body of Christ is, as Paul conceives it in the Ephesian Letter, to "grow up into Christ" (4:15). More specifically, the goal of the Body is to be so built up by those who are concerned about it (4:11, 12) that all its members may attain to "the unity of the faith and of the knowledge of the Son of God, to mature manhood, to the *measure of the stature of the fullness of Christ*" (4:13). The stature of

Christ, the one *New Man,* is what is sought. And this stature, Paul points out, can never be achieved unless two things happen. First, each member must contribute to the life and functioning of the Body what it alone, whether "joint or sinew," is capable of giving (4:16). Secondly, all action must be co-ordinated. The members of the Body must realize that they are "members one of another"; they must accordingly act together "in love" for the good of the whole. On the one hand each member of the Body shall function in accordance with its nature. This it shall do as an individual, expressing in the fullest sense its individuality, but without any tinge of individualism. On the other hand, the activity of the parts must be harmonized with the action which the Body as a whole undertakes to perform. As a member of the Body of Christ every Christian is important and must work; but the work he undertakes should be in the spirit of love, with consideration and appreciation for the work of other members. In this way a Christian's efforts become part of the total action proposed and undertaken by the Body of Christ, in response to the mandate of the Head, and as an expression of the single life which inspires the Body as a whole. This is the goal of all Christian activity, as it is also the perennial Christian problem, to make all Christians work and at the same time to harmonize the ardor of the separate workers, whether individually or as Churches, with the needs and aims of the whole Christian community as the Body of Christ.

c) THE GREAT UNITIES

Consideration of the Church as a Body leads us immediately and naturally to consider the presentation which Paul makes in this great Epistle of the Unities of the Church. There are seven things which make the Church one. Let us listen as Paul recounts them one by one. "There is one body and one Spirit, just as you were called to the one hope that belongs to your call, one Lord, one faith, one baptism, one God and Father of us all, which is above all and through all, and in all" (4:4–6).

These seven basic unities fall into three groups. There is, first, one body, one Spirit, one hope. The formal connection between these is obvious. The one body is vitalized by the one Spirit and moves progressively towards the one hope. Then we have one Lord, one faith, one baptism. Loyalty to the one Lord gives birth to the one faith and is signalized by the one act of baptism. Finally, superior to all, operative through all, and immanent in all, is the one Eternal God and Father, whose gracious purpose ordained, embraces and gives unity to all the other unities.

Three of these unities are clearly of pivotal importance, the *one Body*, the *one Lord*, the *one God*.

One Body. There is but one ultimate community, the People of God. Jesus Christ has but one Body; there is only one Church of Christ. This fact Christians must ever have in mind for the illumination of their faith and the orientation of their practice. Amid the ecclesiastical welter of the Christian centuries all the members of His Body have been equally dear to Jesus Christ, the Head. It is therefore a very unholy and perilous practice to label and pass ultimate judgments upon fellow Christians. The mortal sin against the Body of Christ, the ultimate apostasy against the Head of the Body, is to practice and glorify "schism" for its own sake. The glorification of schism, the transformation of the command to separate from pagans into an injunction to Christians to separate from other Christians who do not agree absolutely with the view of a dissident group, is to "crucify the Son of God afresh and put him to an open shame." Every conscientious dissenter or dissenting group in the Christian Church should be treated with the utmost respect and consideration. But to break the unity of the Body of Christ merely for schism's sake, is to say, "Schism be thou my Good," and to follow in the trail of the "lost archangel." I am speaking here of the canonization of revolt as such and not of the constant necessity of reform within the Christian Church.

Within the Christian community there is *one Spirit*, who was given to the Church for ever. The new life of Christians, their growth in Christ, the manifestation in them of special gifts and graces are due to the presence and work of the Holy Spirit. The Spirit is the foe of strife and the source of concord in the Church. His presence, as the author and perfecter of Christian love, is the special seal of God upon the members of the Community. The most disastrous thing that Christians can do is to "grieve the Holy Spirit." For then "love, joy, peace in the Holy Ghost" disappear, and with them one of the most precious Christian unities.

The Spirit that vivifies the Body makes real and keeps alive the great Christian *hope*. This is the sure hope of salvation, of the ultimate redemption and triumph of the Body, through the power of the Risen Christ. Buoyed up by this hope Christians are "not ashamed"; they wear salvation, "the hope of salvation," as a helmet upon their heads. For that reason they can keep their heads erect when other heads are bowed. They can smile serenely in danger when others quake with terror. They greet the unknown tomorrow with a cheer; for beyond the darkness is the dawn and salvation "draweth nigh."

One Lord. The members of the one Body, vitalized by the one Spirit and inspired by the one hope, give allegiance to one Lord, who is the Head of the Body. The one Lord Jesus Christ is the subject of the Body, controlling its life. He is also the object of the Body's devotion receiving the passionate loyalty of all its members. All the details of practical endeavour they carry on, and all the problems of relationship and behaviour, they solve "in the Lord."

"Jesus Christ is Lord." These are the words of the earliest and most basic Christian creed. In the Letter which he addressed from his Roman prison to the Philippian Church, Paul catches up and re-echoes a formula of Christian devotion which was current in the first century Church. The time was coming, he said, when every tongue would "confess that *Jesus Christ is Lord,* to the glory of God the Father" (Phil. 2:11). Here is the first creed in point of time and the basic creed for all time. "Lord," *Kurios,* was the term used in the Septuagint, the Greek translation of the Old Testament, to designate Jehovah, or Jahweh, the God of Israel. It was also the current term used in the world of St. Paul to designate the Roman Emperor. This same term, *Kurios,* the Apostle uses two hundred and fifty times in his writings to designate the *One Lord,* Jesus Christ, who was very God and mightier than imperial Caesar, in whose prison, he, Paul was "Christ's ambassador in chains."

At this point we pause. To say truly that "Jesus Christ is Lord" is to make the basic affirmation of the Christian religion. "No man," said Paul, "can say that Jesus is the Lord but by the Holy Ghost" (I Cor. 12:3). Yet to make this affirmation as a cold conceptual formula of scholastic orthodoxy does not make one a Christian. Many, as Jesus Himself said, may say to Him, "Lord, Lord"; but the One Lord will not acknowledge them because He was never the Lord of their lives. This greatest of Christian unities becomes real, we become Christians in the New Testament sense, members of the one Body, when, in the totality of our selfhood, we bow ourselves adoringly before the living reality of Jesus Christ the Lord. Jesus Christ the Lord is not honored when we affirm a conceptual truth regarding Him for the sake of orthodox standing. He is honored only when we submit ourselves to His sovereign sway who alone can give us vital being. To rediscover in this time of new "lords" and passionate loyalties all that is involved in the timeless creed that Jesus Christ is Lord, would be to recover the atmosphere and recreate the reality of the Apostolic age.

To make Jesus King over life in its wholeness, to contend with all who dispute His "crown rights," to reject the idea that He has abdicated and left to other "lords" the conduct of affairs in His Church, this is the great unity of action which corresponds to the unity of faith in the "One Lord." Both as the one and only Head of the Church, and as the supreme court of Christian appeal, Jesus Christ is Lord.

Allegiance to Jesus Christ as the *One Lord* gives birth to *One Faith*. The question is asked insistently, "What are the essentials of the Christian faith?" In a formal sense, the question is easy to answer. The essentials of the Christian faith are those affirmations of belief which center in, and derive from, the basic Christian conviction that Jesus Christ is Lord. Within the context and atmosphere of the Ephesian Letter this means that Jesus Christ is at the center of the "Mystery," the great scheme of redemption which God has revealed. No one can know what Jesus Christ and His lordship really mean save in the context of Holy Scripture. For Jesus Christ is in the fullest sense the Lord of the Scriptures, the clue to their meaning, and the core of their message. That being so, any statement of essential Christian belief that would be expressive of, and loyal to, the One Faith must include first the acceptance of the supreme authority of the Bible as the Word of God where alone we learn about Jesus Christ; second, an adequate statement based upon the Bible concerning Jesus Christ and the great events and truths that center in him; third, the acceptance of the two Sacraments instituted by Christ, Baptism and the Lord's Supper. Some would add the acceptance of some particular affirmation regarding Church Order, for example, the "Historic Episcopate." I do not feel, however, that any formulation relating to the form, as against the substance and spirit, of Church Order, belongs to the essence of the *One Faith*. This point will receive fuller elucidation in the next section.

At present, the revived interest in Christian theology and the historic Christian faith, and the many endeavors to bring about Church union, give great actuality to a discussion of the *One Faith*. Certain things may be affirmed.

One: There can be no Christian unity, nor should there be consummated any Christian union, that is not based upon unqualified loyalty to the One Lord. The constitution of the World Council of Churches which was organized in Amsterdam in August 1948, in making the basis of membership in the Council the acceptance by all member Churches, of "Jesus Christ as God and Saviour," establishes the foundational loyalty from which all negotiations between Churches for closer relations must take their departure. This basis, let it be observed, would not be nor was it ever intended to be an adequate basis for organic Church union. It was intended merely to be a basis upon which Churches might stand in order to worship God together, to think together, as far as possible to speak and act together, and at the very least to discuss their differences together.

Two: No motive of expediency, no political pressure, no search for greater corporate power, no idealistic sentiment, no financial interest, no social concern or cultural affinity, can provide a worthy or adequate ground for the union of Christian Churches. Such union must always be union in the Truth. Therefore, all movements towards Church unity, and the organization of every Church union, must recognize the august majesty of Truth. Truth must always be a prior concern to unity. But I hasten to add this: Let it never be forgotten that Jesus Christ is the Truth, that Christian unity is a part of the Christian truth, and that all truth must be held and spoken in love.

Three: Moved by a concern for the *One Faith*, and dedicated to achieve the maximum visible unity of the *One Body*, all Christian Churches should re-examine themselves. In loyalty to the *One Lord*, guided by the *One Spirit*, and pressing forward towards the *One Hope*, they should inquire what it is that Jesus Christ gave them as a unique witness, or as a special gift or grace, which they would desire, in all humility and for the sake of Christ's Body the Church, to bring as their contribution to a larger Christian unity.

Four: The quality and success of any church union that may be consummated will depend, not only upon the Christian Spirit and devotion of those who enter into it, but also upon the rich foundations of Christian truth upon which it is established. The richer and more adequate the confessional statement of faith upon which Churches unite, provided always that the doctrinal affirmations are intelligently and enthusiastically endorsed, the more cohesive will be their unity in the *One Faith*; and the greater will be the treasures of common belief upon which they can draw for their educational task. A creedless Church, or a Church with a very thin creed, is confronted with the difficulty which arises when a Church lacks an adequate doctrinal basis for its cultural task.

Five: One of the greatest needs of the *One Faith* in our time is that the Christian Church should devote itself to the task of elaborating an ecumenical theology. In this epoch when the world is physically united and spiritually rifted; when the clash of secular "faiths" resounds on every frontier of the globe; when the Christian Church is truly ecumenical, being coextensive with the inhabited earth; when the majestic splendor of God's purpose in Christ Jesus breaks afresh upon the Christian mind, the time is ripening for a theological statement which would take these diverse factors into account. But to repeat words which I have written elsewhere, never must the Church of Christ sponsor a blanched, eviscerated, spineless statement of confessional theology. It must give birth in this revolutionary transition time to a full-blooded, loyally Biblical, unashamedly ecumenical, and strongly vertebrate system of Christian belief.

Those who serve the *One Lord* and profess the *One Faith* make public acknowledgement of the same by submitting to the rite of *Baptism*. Baptism is one of the sacraments instituted by Jesus Christ whereby, by the symbolical use of water to signify cleansing from sin and the identification of the baptized person with Jesus Christ in his death and resurrection, the Christian believer is incorporated into the Church of Christ as a visible community. Christians, Paul says, are "baptized unto Christ" (Rom. 6:3;

Gal. 3:27). Or, which means the same thing, "all are baptized into one Body," that is, into the Church of Christ as a collective personality, into the New Humanity. Baptized persons, therefore, who have been baptized in the name of the Father, the Son, and the Holy Ghost, whatever their age when they were baptized, or the form or circumstances of their baptism, stand before the world as belonging to the Christian Church. Baptism involves, by its very nature, a break with one's old life and relationships and an overt commitment to Christ, to the Church and to a new life. The baptized person must then make a stand, otherwise his baptism has no significance whatever.

In the Christian Church today, the radical significance and consequences of Christian baptism on the New Testament model become most dramatically apparent when individuals or families belonging to a non-Christian faith, or who live in a secularized community hostile to the Christian faith, decide to profess their faith in Jesus Christ by baptism. In such cases baptism may be followed by the repudiation of the baptized person by their kinsfolk and local community, and even by severe discrimination and active persecution. So long as a person holds his beliefs and sympathies to himself, so long as he makes no official profession of his faith and is not received by baptism into the ranks of the Christian Church, nothing happens to him. He pays the price of believing only when his faith is sealed by the water of baptism.

How lamentable it is that, in a wide sector of the Christian Church today, the inherent New Testament meaning of baptism has ceased to have significance. In some circles the Sacrament has come to connote a magical rite whereby a baptized infant is regenerated by the Holy Spirit. Such a view not only violates the whole spirit of Biblical religion, it produces besides a spirit of complacency and irresponsibility in millions of Christians. In other circles, while the idea of baptismal regeneration may not be accepted, baptism becomes reduced to a purely formal rite. It is the first of a series of rites which, when they have been performed, guarantee to the person who has passed through the whole series, good and regular standing in the Christian Church. It matters nothing whether the person in question is a living, active member of the Church or not. He may put in an appearance in a Christian sanctuary once a year, or even less frequently. He has *graduated* from Church. As a Church "graduate," or "alumnus," his active Christian commitment may mean no more than a sentimental interest in the institution which gave him his several ecclesiastical diplomas. It was the overpowering awareness that millions of baptized people in Europe had no interest whatever in Jesus Christ or the Church, which led Karl Barth to make a violent attack upon the whole baptismal system as practised today by many Christian Churches. He wanted to infuse the *One Baptism, one God and Father of all* with pristine, Biblical meaning.

All the other unities come into being through, are inspired by, and serve the eternal purpose of, the most basic unity of all: *God, the Universal,* the *"Archetypal Father."* "From Him the whole family in heaven and earth—despite the diversity and historical divergences and conflicts between its members—is named." God, the "Father Everlasting," is alone permanent amid all the vicissitudes of cosmic and earthly life. Man's creations appear and dissolve, his empires rise and fall, his civilizations wax and wane, but God's timeless purpose in Jesus Christ, to "sum up all things in Him," abides constant through all change. "To Him be glory in the Church and in Christ Jesus to all generations for ever and ever" (Eph. 3:21).

Only when the Christian view of God is taken seriously, and men become aware of the Being and the Purpose which are operative in history, is there any hope for the realization of many a cherished human longing. Internationalism and the desire for human brotherhood, apart from faith in the divine Fatherhood, are futile dreams which become tragic failures. Brotherhood cannot be achieved by simply willing it. No human sentiment, love, least of all, can be created by an act of will. The love which makes men brothers must grow naturally and spontaneously out of a sense of a common relationship to a Father who loves all men. Love is of God; men must be planted in the soil of love or they cannot grow unto love, whether upwards towards God or outwards towards one another.

How painful and ironic is the thought that the epoch in history when men talked most about brotherhood was an epoch marked by two world wars. But for Christians "the things which cannot be shaken" still remain. Chief among these is the experienced certainty that the Eternal God, the God and Father of Jesus Christ, is our God and Father, too. It is meet, therefore, in this most tragic time, to re-echo in faith and in hope, the rhapsody of adoration with which Paul began the Ephesian Letter. "Blessed be the God and Father of our Lord Jesus Christ, who has blessed us in Christ with every spiritual blessing in the heavenly places." In the spirit of David in a woeful moment of his life, and adapting the words of the monarch bard of Israel, let us repeat today, "Though our house—the house of the Christian Church and of our common humanity—be not so with God, yet hath He made with us an everlasting Covenant, ordered in all things and sure. This is all our salvation and all our desire" (II Sam. 23:5).

CHAPTER VII

The Fullness of Christ

But how is the unity of the Church to be achieved? How are the great unities of the faith which were considered in the last chapter to express themselves?

Paul now proceeds to answer these questions. He answers them by saying that Christ, out of His fullness, as the Head of the Church, gives to the Church as special gifts men whom He has endued with the gifts and qualifications necessary to fit them for their several tasks. Jesus Christ, the mighty Conqueror who first descended into the lower regions of terrestrial experience and need, and then ascended to the seat of celestial power, now bestows a diversity of gifts from His heavenly largess (Eph. 4:7–10).

a) OUT OF HIS FULLNESS—GIFTED MEN

What were the gifts of Christ? His gifts were that some should be "apostles, some prophets, some evangelists, some pastors and teachers" (4:11). These were all "ministers," "servants" of God and of the Church. They were to have a relationship to the Church at large in the same way that "bishops," "presbyters," and "deacons" were to have special responsibility for particular regions or local churches.

In the forefront of Christ's human gifts to His Church Paul places *"apostles."* The apostles were His "special Messengers." They were men who could bear witness to the fact that the Humiliated One who had descended became the Risen One who ascended "far above all heavens." Most apostles had seen Christ and heard Him, had followed Him and handled Him during His earthly career. Paul himself had not known Christ "in the days of His flesh." However, the Risen and Ascended One, after His earthly career with its attendant humiliation had come to a close, met Paul and addressed him in dramatic circumstances, giving him at the same time the commission of an "apostle." Yet Paul and his fellow apostles were not men of conceptual genius. They were not gifted with the capacity to penetrate into the inner meaning of reality and of universal history. They were not in the classical tradition of "philosophers and wise people" who could weave complicated textures of thought, world-views spun out of their inner consciousness. They were on the whole rather ordinary men. But they had been given unusual perceptual opportunities. They could bear concrete witness to the facts that lay behind the affirmation of the first Christian community, "Jesus Christ is Lord." The apostles were perceptual witnesses to the fact that the Crucified One became the Risen One.

"Prophets," who constituted the second group of gifted men, took the affirmation of the apostles regarding the resurrection and Lordship of Christ and interpreted its meaning. They themselves were a proof of the fact stated by the writer of the Apocalypse "that the testimony of Jesus is the spirit of prophecy" (Rev. 19:10). They were enabled, under the guidance of the Spirit, to engage in solid Christian thinking in the light and in the terms of the Risen Lord to whom the apostles bore witness. The "prophets," their minds illumined by Christ the Truth, showed deep

insight into the meaning of Christ. They could discern times and seasons, they could interpret God to man and man to himself. Some of them wrote books which have a place in the New Testament canon. Their successors down the Christian ages have been creed-makers and theologians, the true succession of New Testament thinkers. Today the sons of those "prophets" wrestle with the task of presenting Christian truth to a highly sophisticated and secularized generation. They aim to do so in such a way that "the truth as it is in Jesus" shall be set forth in the categories which are native to it, and which, at the same time, shall challenge the men and women, lettered or unlearned, primitive savage or priggish Athenian, who are natives of the twentieth century.

Third in the succession of Christ's gifts are the *"evangelists."* Evangelists are men specially gifted to be preachers of the Gospel, "the Good News," regarding the Crucified and Risen One. The evangelist takes the truth to which the apostle bears witness, and which the prophet interprets, and proclaims it as the Good News. The task of the evangelist has been admirably set forth in a document of the contemporary church. It is "so to present Jesus Christ in the power of the Holy Ghost that men shall come to put their trust in God through Him, to accept Him as their Saviour and follow Him as their King, in the fellowship of His Church." [1] The Christian evangelist feels himself commissioned to go to all men, in every land where they live, and in every place where they work. He will address them with passionate conviction and crystaline clarity. He will in every instance look for the best approach to the people he seeks to convert, recognizing the fact that his first great task is to win a right to be heard. If he wins that right, he will not rest satisfied until he is understood and his message is obeyed. In the pursuit of that goal it will be the constant aspiration of the true evangelist that the foreign word in his message shall become indigenous flesh. The one thing above all else which he will seek is a serious response to his message. He will constantly

---

[1] *Towards the Conversion of England.*

seek to reproduce that classical emblem of surrender to the Lord of Life commonly known as "Calvin's crest," in which appears a flaming heart in an outstretched hand, and the interpretive words, "My heart I give thee, Lord, eagerly and sincerely." Commitment to Jesus Christ is what the contemporary successor of the early order of evangelists will continue to pursue.

"*Pastors*" are also the gift of Christ. They are men to whom he has given the shepherd's heart, who are followers of the great Shepherd Himself, who like Paul, love men "in the bowels," that is, "with the affection" of Jesus Christ. Other religions have their prophets and priests, and even their evangelists, but only the Christian religion has produced an order of shepherds. The Christian pastor, with his shepherd's heart and his pastoral vocation, is unique among religious functionaries. In the end it is the Christian pastor and he alone who will prove a match for the fiery devotees of Marxist Communism. For the time will come when broken and disillusioned men, flaming revolutionaries of yesterday and today, with lights gone out and fires quenched, will need the tenderness of the shepherd's heart. Their hopes of a new era shattered, and being oppressed by the unlooked for phenomenon of post-revolutionary evil, they will seek men who love them as individuals, who will restore their souls, shepherding them in "green pastures" beside "still waters." For the lonely and broken human spirit there is no help nor hope but a man with a shepherd's heart who finds him in prison, or as a wayfaring waif on the road of life.

After the pastors come the "*teachers.*" Teachers in the great evangelical succession are men and women who, taking those who have entered upon a new spiritual experience through the work of the evangelist, and whose new life is being nurtured by the pastor, instruct them in the Christian faith. This is the great task of Christian education. It involves instruction in the Bible and in the meaning and implications of the Christian faith. The teacher must do much more than present Christian truths factually and theologically; he must teach people how to be Christian in every circumstance and walk of life. A very large part of Christian education consists in taking people who belong to the several vocations of life and showing them how to think and live and act like Christians in their secular calling. A Christian teacher has no greater task than to make explicit the meaning of the Bible and of the Christian life in all the spheres of daily work and in all the phases of human experience. The Christian teacher must help people to "learn Christ," so that all life may become Christian. The goal of Christian instruction will be to guide all thinking into the obedience of Christ, to bring every sphere under the law of Christ.

b) TOWARDS HIS FULLNESS—AN EFFECTIVE MINISTRY

Men whom Christ has specially gifted, and who become His gift to the Church, have one great task in common. They must exercise their ministry in such a way that the "saints" shall be "perfected" or "equipped," in order that they too, in a non-professional but effective sense, may become "ministers." In this way and only in this way shall the whole Body of Christ be built up (4:13).

No passage in the Bible is more crucial than this for the welfare and mission of the Christian Church today. The familiar translation of this important passage runs thus: "And he gave some, apostles; and some, prophets; and some, evangelists; and some, pastors and teachers; for the perfecting of the saints, for the work of the ministry, for the edifying of the Body of Christ" (4:11, 12). In the recently published Revised Standard Version the passage is rendered "for the equipment of the saints, for the work of ministry, for building up the Body of Christ." Here, without linguistic authority but with undoubted ecclesiological bias, the fatal comma after the word "saints" has been retained. Churchmen balk at sanctioning a New Testament "ministry" for ordinary Christians. Yet, according to some of the best and most modern New Testament scholarship, and some most reputable translations of the New Testament, such as Weymouth's and Phillips', the obvious meaning of the passage is simply this, namely, that the "saints" are "equipped" to serve. J. B. Phillips, in his *Letters to Young Churches*, which is a translation of the New Testament epistles, has this free rendering, "His gifts were made that Christians might be properly equipped for their service, that the whole Body might be built up." [2] Richard Francis Weymouth in his famous translation of the New Testament, *The New Testament in Modern Speech*, thus rendered the passage in question, "In order fully to equip his people for the work of serving for the building up of Christ's Body."

In favor of this rendering is not only the general tenor of Paul's thought in his Epistle to the Ephesians and of his general view of special Church functionaries, but also the usage of the Greek prepositions involved. While the preposition *pros,* meaning "with a view to," is used before the preparation or the equipment of the saints, a different preposition of similar meaning, *eis,* "to the end that," is used before each of the two phrases, the work of ministering, and the building up of the Body. The meaning appears clearly to be that the supreme objective of the gifted men must be to equip the "saints" that they, in their turn, may engage in ministering, that they too may be servants, and that resulting from their service the Body of Christ may be built up.

The whole idea is startling, but decisive. The supreme function of the so-called officers of the Church whose ministry is related to some aspect of the Church's welfare may be defined thus: It is the function of "ministers" so to equip the "saints," that is, members of the rank and file of the Christian congregation who are, by their commitment and profession, "Christ's men and women," that they too may render service to Christ and the Church in the fullest sense of the term. Members of the laity are under the same obligation as members of the clergy to be utterly Christian, to

---

[2] Published by The Macmillan Company in 1950.

take seriously their Christian calling, and to follow in the steps of Him who said that "He came not to be ministered unto, but to minister." For the formation of their Christian spirit and the guidance of their Christian service, lay men and women must keep constantly before them the essential image of the Christian religion. That essential image is given us in St. John's Gospel, Chapter 13:1–17. Jesus, intensely aware of His identity and His destiny, and that absolute power was His, "that the Father had given all things into His hands," and that He was about to return to God from whence He had come, poured water into a basin and, girt with a towel, washed and dried His disciples' feet. This is the authoritative pattern for all the "saints." Aware of the fact that they are heirs of God and joint heirs with Christ, "Christ's men and women" must be ready at all times to perform the most menial tasks in the service of Christ and of their fellowmen. They must dedicate their powers and their talents, their time and their money, their status and their reputation, to fulfilling their Christian vocation and to building up the Christian community which is the Body of Christ. They who have "ascended" with Christ, who are "in Christ" and so live "in the heavenly places in Christ Jesus," must also descend, as He did, into "the lowest part of the earth," that is, if they are to take seriously the injunction that their Christian thought and action must be carried on "in the Lord."

What we have here been considering is nothing more nor less than a facet of the basic New Testament truth of *the universal priesthood of believers*. Every Christian is called to be a minister, a servant, a priest. His supreme offering must be the offering of himself and his service to Christ and to men. Such an offering cannot be rendered by proxy. It can only be rendered by himself and in such a way that the reality of the foot-washing, the pain of the Cross, and the power of the Resurrection shall all enter into it. It is one of the very sad things in Christian history that the doctrine of the universal priesthood of believers has been too often and too long interpreted as the mere affirmation of the rights and privileges of every Christian to approach Jesus Christ "within the veil" and to enjoy the fullest share of spiritual blessing. It is time for Christians to become aware that priesthood means responsibility as well as privilege. The Christian priest must show that he prizes his privileges by accepting his responsibilities, by offering himself and seeking to offer others as living sacrifices upon the altar of Christian devotion. It is not enough that a Christian, whether a member of the clergy or the laity, should do good to other people in the spirit of Jesus Christ; it should be his constant aim that they who become the recipients of good should themselves become doers of good. He will not, of course, lay it down as a condition of the good he does that those who benefit from his goodness should reciprocate by doing what he asks them to do. For a Christian to proceed thus would be to act out of "theological charity," whereby the recipient of goodness would become obliged to conform himself to the ideas and precepts laid down by his benefactor. Nevertheless, while abhorring all semblance of "theological charity," the supreme goal of all Christian service must be that those who are served shall give their own lives to the Christ in whose name, by whose grace, and for whose glory all true service is rendered.

A word is called for regarding "saints" and "sainthood." The word "saint" is a term which has been greatly misunderstood and travestied through the ages. There are few Biblical terms to which the twentieth century is more allergic. Most people totally misunderstand the meaning of Christian sainthood. Many others who understand it have an antipathy to its implications. Saints in the New Testament are not people distinguished for their ascetic practices in the control of their bodies, nor yet for their spiritual capacity for mystic flights and raptures. They are simply and solely, as they have been called, "Christ's men and women." Feeling that they belong to Christ, they recognize the privilege and accept the obligation of carrying out in their lives the uttermost implications of being Christian. Some of them will scale the mystic ladder and will otherwise, by the special grace of Christ, achieve "sainthood" in the more traditional sense of the term. But all those who take their Christian vocation seriously, and who strive to be "saints" in the New Testament sense, are the true humanists; for it is they and only they who strive to be truly human and have any possibility of achieving that kind of manhood which flows from the fullness of Christ. A person is a "saint" in the New Testament sense not by the greatness of his spiritual achievement but by the reality of his Christian devotion.

When every "saint" takes his call to sainthood seriously, expressing in thought and life all the implications of belonging to Jesus Christ, the Church which is the Body of Christ will be truly built up. Every member will be in health and will perform his especial function. Then, under the leaders appointed by Christ, and recognized by the congregation for the conduct of the Church's life, the Body as a whole will function harmoniously in obedience to Christ, and will be equipped for the corporate service of Christ.

The Meaning of Church Order

I venture to pause at this point to offer some reflections on the question of the Christian ministry and of Church order; for the passage which has just engaged our attention is crucial for the Christian understanding of both.

Christians who accept the centralities of the New Testament faith and are loyal to the unities which we dealt with in the last chapter, very seriously differ on the relationship between Church order, including the ministry, to the Christian faith and its basic reality. The view which is here taken is that in the Church of Jesus Christ Order is order. This means that in the Christian Church structure is essentially functional in character. The functionaries of the Church, and the form of its organization, have been designed by Jesus Christ to serve the best interests of the

Church, to fulfill His purpose for the Church. That purpose consists, as we shall see more fully later, in the preparation of all Church members to fulfill to the very utmost their several functions and to grow up together unto the measure of the stature of Christ's fullness. What the Head of the Church has designed for the members of His Body and for the Body as a whole is the fullest spiritual maturity. That being so, while we are provided in the New Testament with a pattern for Church leadership and organization, both of these must ultimately be judged by the measure in which they contribute to "equipping the saints for the work of ministering and for the building up of the Body of Christ." The moment an ecclesiastical functionary, or a specific form of church order, fails to make it its aim to form mature Christians and to make the Church as a whole a usable instrument of the will of Christ, an aberration takes place from the spirit, and I venture to say also, from the letter of New Testament teaching, regarding the Church and its ministry.

There are two views in particular of the Church and the ministry which appear to be in opposition to the view that is implicit in the Ephesian Letter. One of these views might be formulated thus: *Order is the Church*. This is the Roman Catholic view. It is held that the clergy, and in particular the hierarchs who control the Church, belong to the Church in a sense that ordinary Catholic believers do not. The Church in its institutional form is to all intents and purposes the hierarchy and the organizational structure which is constituted by the hierarchs. The hierarchy *is* the Church. It owns the Church and regards itself as vested with divine authority to shape the destinies of the Church. More and more in modern Roman Catholic literature it is affirmed that Jesus Christ founded his "Organization." The Church as an institution rather than as a fellowship constitutes, in this view, the basic reality of the Christian Church. If that is so, then certain functionaries and a certain structural pattern constitute the Church.

This particular view of the Church has produced two sinister results. For all practical purposes, so far as ordinary human beings are concerned, the Church takes the place of Deity. Christ and the Church become so institutionally one that there is no longer any possibility of appeal from the institutional Church to Jesus Christ. The Head of the Church loses His sovereignty. The Church becomes His patron, presuming to control His movements and His gracious influence. The same situation obtained with disastrous results, in the religious history of Israel, when the presence and living power of God were mechanically identified with the existence of the Ark and later with the Temple. The Christian Church is something more and greater than the institution called The Church. Jesus Christ is more and greater than the Church in any form.

This view of the nature of Church order produces another evil. Where Order becomes the Church there emerges a sinister reality called Clericalism. Roman Clericalism I have already defined as "the pursuit of power, especially political power, by a religious hierarchy, carried on by secular methods and for purposes of social domination." It is based upon the affirmation that the institutional Church, constituted by its hierarchy, is the Kingdom of God, and so an end in itself. For that reason, the interests of the Church, which are identical with the interests of the hierarchy, constitute the supreme goal to be pursued. The ideal social situation in history thus becomes one in which the people of a nation, and also their rulers, subject their thinking and their actions to what the Church considers to be right in the best interests of men and of the Church. The development of Clericalism invests the Church with spiritual sovereignty and creative majesty. The important thing now becomes not that ordinary people should become spiritually mature, but that they should obey the Church. The Church as a substitute for that spiritual maturity which is inseparable from freedom, gives is members that kind of security which is the death of freedom. The rank and file of the faithful become eternal children. Faith is no longer faith in Christ. It becomes assent to propositions regarding Him. It is related especially to belief in the authority which Christ vested in the Church. So absolute is this authority that it proclaims as articles of faith that certain events took place as objective historical facts, although neither history nor Scripture nor tradition records the events. The Church thus has power to create events of historical and cosmic import, and need not confine its action to bearing witness to the mighty acts of God.

The other view of the Church which also runs counter to the spirit and teaching of the Ephesian Letter is the view which regards *Order as an article of faith,* that is, as belonging to the essence of the Church. This is the view ordinarily associated with the Eastern Orthodox Church and with the High Church branch of the Anglican Communion. This view of the Church, which is held by many conscientious and saintly people, makes it difficult for them to accept the ministerial orders of other churches whose ministry may have been singularly blessed by the presence and power of the Holy Spirit. Members of such churches will not allow others to participate with them in their celebration of Holy Communion, nor will they allow their people to partake of the Sacrament of the Lord's Supper under the auspices of Protestant churches. In this view the Free Churches are "societies" rather than Churches. This is the view of the Church which constitutes a major obstacle to the union of younger churches in the so-called mission fields of the world. A Christian poet like T. S. Eliot, to whom both poetry and Christian culture in our time owe a deep debt of gratitude, has allowed himself, because of his high-churchism, to designate such an eminently Christian achievement as the constitution of a new united Church in South India as "an amiable masquerade," "an elaborate artifice," "a pantomime horse."

The peril of such a view of the Church is Churchism. The institutional church whose ministers regard themselves to be the successors of the apostles, tends to become an end in itself. It promotes vested institutional interests rather than the evangelical interests of Jesus Christ, of the saints, and of the Kingdom of God. In Churchism, the Church presumes to possess a monopoly of the Holy Spirit, just as in Clericalism it becomes the patron of the Risen Christ.

Over against Clericalism and Churchism stands the view, New Testament and Pauline, that the Church as the new Israel needs no specific institutional structure, or a special order of hierarchs, to guarantee its sacred origin or to make efficacious its God-given task. For such a man as John Calvin the Presbyterian form of Church order was the one that expressed most truly the New Testament pattern. Calvin hastened, however, to add that in his view other Christians could, without doing violence to the New Testament, find other forms of ecclesiastical organization in its sacred pages. Who in the light of the New Testament, the specific teaching of the Ephesian Letter, and the record of Christian history, would dare affirm that the Holy Spirit of God has exhausted structural possibilities for the Christian Church? In the contemporary situation loyalty to Christ and the Church and to the spirit of the Ephesian Letter demands that we envision ecclesiastical order as being essentially functional in character. That order is best in a given time and environment which is most fully loyal to the spirit of the New Testament Church and most perfectly "equips the saints for ministering." Order is order and structure is structure. What is required is this. Let Christians who are rooted in the Bible and committed to Jesus Christ the living Word of God, and who proclaim the Gospel of His grace, be so related to one another that souls shall be born into the faith of Christ, nurtured in the life of Christ, and knit together in the spirit of Christ. Only thus can they attain that degree of spiritual maturity which becomes possible through the fullness of Christ. For the only form of ecclesiastical order which can reflect, or be continuous with, the New Testament Church is one which produces saints and cultivates the communion of saints.

c) THE REALIZATION OF HIS FULLNESS— CHRISTIAN MATURITY

The Christian pattern of life is mature manhood. The success or failure of Church leaders will, as we have seen, be measured by the degree in which they contribute to the formation of Christian maturity in those to whom they minister. In the measure in which Christian maturity is achieved the fullness of Christ will be manifest and consummated. The gifts and graces which Christ bestows out of His fullness for the building up of His Body the Church will, let us say it with all reverence, contribute towards His own fullness through the growth and perfection of that Body. To build up the Body of Christ and to achieve Christian maturity are inseparably related. The maturity of individual Christians cannot be realized apart from their growth in the Body and their personal contribution, in unison with other Christians, to the growth of the Body. On the other hand, the Body as a whole cannot grow apart from the growth and harmonious functioning of its members. Christian manhood and the communion of saints cannot be separated.

But the interests of individual Christians and those of the corporate body of Christians can be reconciled only when the truth is held in love. Truth is something which an individual Christian passionately feels and something to which he wants to devote himself. But let him beware lest, in standing for the Truth, he be not more interested in achieving pre-eminence as a witness to the Truth than in the cause of Truth itself. It is easy, and it often flatters human pride, to be able to make a case. It is much more difficult to lose one's self in a cause. Let the Christian be careful lest he should confuse the cause of Truth with the attempt to consolidate his own position and to insure his own prestige. Above all, let him not allow the partial truth for which he stands to go mad with that kind of madness to which our generation has become accustomed in the political order. The only way in which a Christian can avoid truth going mad, and prevent himself becoming a fanatical devotee of a partial truth, is that the truth be "held in love." For when the truth is held in love two things happen. It is recognized that love itself is a part, and a very basic part, of Christian truth. Secondly, it is impossible to hold the truth in love without having a sense of Christian wholeness. By speaking the truth in love we have regard for fellow Christians who with ourselves belong to the Body of Christ, who are fully loyal to Christ, the Head, but who feel constrained to emphasize some aspect of truth which is different from the aspect which is supremely important to us.

Only when the principle of speaking the truth in love is loyally adhered to can Christians avoid that immaturity which we associate with children. Adolescents become fanatically devoted to partial truths. Christians must no longer be children "who are tossed to and fro and are carried about with every wind of doctrine by the cunning of men, by their craftiness and deceitful wiles" (Eph. 4:14). Rather, says Paul, "speaking the truth in love, we are to grow up in every way into Him who is the Head, into Christ" (4:15). Nothing is more disastrous than that sincere Christians, in their zeal for Christian truth, should fall a prey to men of "clever and unscrupulous cunning." Such men are skilled in "the crafty presentation of lies"; they distort and pervert the truth; they wrest it from its natural context; they gloat over every manifestation of schism in the Christian Church. Sometimes in whispers and sometimes in fierce waves of propaganda, they try to rally adolescent Christians to their banner. Members of the "Younger Churches" are particularly exposed to this kind of diabolical craft which regards schism as a virtue and the manifestation of Christian unity as apostasy. Men who prey upon the adolescent Christian mind in order to embitter it against

Christians who take seriously the New Testament injunction that unity in the love and service of Christ is part of the Christian truth, stand in the Biblical tradition of "enemies of the Cross of Christ." Such people are modern sons of the lost Archangel whose consuming passion was to disrupt the divine harmony, writing upon his crusading banner the tremendous slogan, "Evil be thou my Good." Such influences assaulted the Christians of Paul's time in the legalistic prescriptions of the Judaizers and the ideological formulations of the Gnostics. For Paul the only true antidote to both was to "learn Christ."

The goal towards which the members of the Body, and the Body as a whole, must strive is the "fullness of Christ." All personal and collective striving must be directed towards "that measure of development which is meant by the fullness of Christ" (Eph. 4:13, Phillips' trans.). Thus the "fullness of Christ" is the end as it was the beginning. How is this fullness to be achieved and what are its manifestations?

To answer this question we bring into focus gleams of spiritual truth which have flashed at different points in the preceding part of the Letter and whose significance achieves its full effulgence at this point. Christ becomes manifest in His fullness through spiritual power. This spiritual power flows from a double unity on the part of Christians; a unity in faith and in the knowledge of the Son of God, and a unity in love.

There is first *unity in knowledge or insight*. Spiritual growth into "the measure of the stature of the fullness of Christ" depends upon insight into, and commitment to, God's eternal purpose to constitute in Christ a new order which shall embrace things on earth and things in heaven. It involves insight into and commitment to the fact that Jesus Christ by His Cross became a spiritual victor who united God and man and Jew and Gentile in a new sense. In the words of the great prayer with which Paul brings to a close the first chapter of the Letter (1:15–23), it is essential that Christians should have "a spirit of wisdom and of revelation in the knowledge of Christ" (1:17). In this way their "hearts," that is their entire personalities, shall be so illumined that they may grasp the meaning of the hope to which they look forward, and what it is going to mean to Jesus Christ to have the saints as His glorious inheritance. It will become theirs also to know, conceptually and by experience, what the great power of God is which became manifest in the resurrection of Christ. This power led to the enthronement of Christ over "all rule and authority and power and dominion and above every name that is named not only in this age but also in that which is to come." They will come to know what it means that Christ has been made "Head over all things for the Church." For that Church is the Body of Christ; it becomes the fullness of Christ who fills the Universe entirely. The vision of this great divine drama and that kind of power which is experienced when people become actors in this drama are indispensable if the fullness of Christ is to be made manifest. That is to say, a common faith, a common knowledge, a common experience, a common power, are indispensable if God's purpose in Jesus Christ to display Christ's fullness in time and beyond time, is to be fulfilled.

Equally important is *unity in love*. In the great prayer with which the third chapter concludes (3:14-21), Paul makes clear that, as the minds of Christians must be illumined by the Holy Spirit for the great vision of truth which centers in God's purpose in Christ, so, too, the Spirit must strengthen the inmost structure of their being in order that there at the center of their personality, Christ Himself may dwell. For it is only in the measure that Christ Himself dwells in the hearts of Christians that they, "being rooted and grounded in love may have power to comprehend with all the saints what is the breadth, and length and height and depth, and to know the love of Christ which surpasses knowledge." Only so, through a corporate vision and experience of love, can they be "filled with all the fullness of God." The fullness of Christ is thus a fullness of being, as well as a fullness of knowledge. In this fullness man's immemorial striving to know and to be come to an end; for the fullness of Christ is the consummation both of man's longing and striving, and of God's planning and achieving.

But, if this is the goal, a participation in the "fullness of Christ," what, in the light of this vision, must Christians do? As members of the Church militant how shall they think and live in order that the fullness of Christ may become a reality, and that glimpses of it may become visible in the corporate life of the Christian Church on the road of history?

It is perfectly clear that the fullness of Christ cannot be identified with any historical institution which is called the Church of Christ. That catholicity, that wholeness, which is wide enough to embrace all that belong to Christ as members of His Body is not found within any institutional or visible manifestation of that Body. If we are able to seek the fullness of Christ, we must be interested in every person everywhere who acknowledges Christ, who has been born again by the Spirit of Christ, and whose life bears the marks of Christ. Evangelical catholicity is the only true catholicity, that form of catholicity whose motto is, "Where Christ is, there is the Church." Our supreme concern must ever be such oneness with Christ that we shall recognize the manifestation of His fullness in lives of Christian devotion wherever they appear. We can be absolutely sure, on the other hand, that wherever the power of Jesus Christ is not manifest, and the marks of Jesus Christ do not appear, and the Spirit of Jesus Christ does not inform the relations of those who profess his name, Christ Himself is not present. His sovereign presence is not confined to "temples made with hands," nor can His sovereign lordship be controlled by any ecclesiastical body or any ecclesiastical functionary. It is the birthright of every Christian soul who finds himself cramped and silenced in an over-institutionalized expression of the Christian religion, to cry out with Blaise Pascal, "To thy tribunal, Lord Jesus, I appeal." For Scripture makes clear the possibility, and history confirms the actuality, that any given church structure, despite its pretentions, may deny Jesus Christ and become apostate from Him.

The secret of Christian thought and life consists in the constant maintenance of closeness to Jesus Christ. It is not enough to keep close to the Bible, even though apart from the Bible we can know nothing about Christ. Christ is the core of the Bible's message and the clue to the Bible's meaning. The Bible fulfills its God-given function when it leads its reader to Christ and builds him up in the faith, and knowledge, and experience of Christ. The moment, however, that the Bible is made a substitute for Christ it becomes an idol. The living Lord Jesus Christ, the Head of the Church, is greater even than the Bible. To make the Bible, apart from Jesus Christ, the object of faith is not only idolatry; it can lead people to deny the reality of Christ while paying lip tribute to Him.

So, too, whenever the Church, instead of Christ the Church's Head, becomes the supreme object of devotion, an equal act of idolatry takes place. Then Christ, and all that He stood for and all that He is, are denied. It is strange, but it is true, that men may become devoted to the Bible and to the Church without being truly Christian. On the other hand, no one whose faith and life are truly Christo-centric, who has a passionate love for and devotion to Jesus Christ, as witnessed to by Holy Scripture, and as constituting the Head of His Body the Church, can ever deny Christ or His truth. Loving Him, they love, for His sake, all fellow Christians in the center of whose faith and life they find the same Crucified and Living Lord.

But the question may be asked, How can Christian knowledge and Christian love so influence Christians in their contact with the secular order, that, as members of the Christian Church, they may think and act in such a way as to contribute to the fullness of Christ? Let Christians baptize unto Christ everything that is truly human in the natural order. That will mean the baptism unto Christ of their secular vocations and callings. All human knowledge and culture should be brought under the light and influence of Christ and be allowed to make their distinctive contribution towards the promotion of the cause of Christ.

This will also mean that in the concrete, everyday life of the Church, Christians must strive to give expression to fellowship with one another and with Christ in worship and in work, within the several denominations and across all denominational bounds. Let them always strive to meet one another at the deepest level, that is, at the level of their common love for Jesus Christ.

In this way, and only in this way, will Christians come to prize that which is true in their own religious heritage and that which is true in the religious heritage of fellow Christians. What is purely conditioned by time will then begin to disappear; the pure gold will be brought into the Christian treasurehouse. Christ Himself, rather than any lesser object, shall become more and more the supreme center of devotion. Christ's fullness shall progressively become manifest and He Himself shall become all and in all. When such a consummation takes place in personal, in institutional, and in denominational life, many a difficult problem in the relations between individuals and churches can and will be solved through the creative working of God's Spirit.

CHAPTER VIII

The Four Imperatives of Christian Living

We have seen Paul soar aloft into realms of truth never before reached by mortal mind; we have seen him touch earth again to speak of unity in the Church, only to take off once more in rhapsodic description of the fullness of Christ. His thought now comes to rest at length on the plane of the horizontal.

In a previous descent upon the runway of life Paul had proclaimed that Christians must live on the roads of life in a way worthy of their calling. This they must do in a humble mood, recognizing a sense of distance between God's greatness and their littleness, and manifesting the while a spirit of meekness, patience, and forebearance towards all fellow Christians. But the moment he mentioned the unity and love which should mark all Christian relationships he took off again on a last soaring flight where we have tried to follow him in the last chapter. After descanting upon the fullness of Christ and its implications for the relations of Christians with one another as members of Christ's Body the Church, he finally settles down to consider the personal behavior of Christian men and women who must live in the world, who have membership in the natural orders of life, in the home and in business, and who must confront the spiritual forces of a demonic, supernatural order. This is where daily life is spent, a place where the Gentiles rule and where Christians must live and struggle until the end of the road.

Thus far Paul has dealt with concepts and figures. He has been thinking, we might say, centrifugally, dealing with the basic truths of Christian thought and experience. He now begins to think in terms of concrete persons. His thought becomes centripetal. He turns from concepts to souls. He shows the ethical implications of the life of God in the soul of man. He insists that the individual who has been called by God and separated unto God must be holy and blameless. He must be devoted, in the truest sense, to good works. For truth is in order to goodness. Goodness must ever be the fruit of the Christian salvation. Pure religion, which consists largely in holy affections for God and for one's fellow Christians, must show itself in true ethical behavior. Moral goodness is the only real proof of a Christian's salvation. Christian truth must produce real persons. It starts from a Person and it must give birth to persons. Christian truth is personal truth in the fullest sense, or it is not truth at all.

Intensely aware once again that he is a prisoner, albeit a prisoner of the Lord, and that Gentiles control the world order, Paul gives counsel to the "saints." He must needs show them how they should behave in a way worthy of their status as men and women who have been called by God to be members of His family. It will not be enough that they should be profoundly versed in the knowledge of God's eternal purpose to found a new order in Christ, nor will it be enough that they should have ecstatic experience of life in the heavenlies. They must even pass beyond the concern to relate themselves with fellow Christians in love as members of the Body of Christ. Neither the sublimities of Christian doctrine, nor the emotion awakened by a personal experience of Christ, nor a sense of the glory of belonging to a fellowship which is at once the Temple, the Bride, and the Body of Christ, should prevent them from taking seriously the problems and concerns of everyday living. The finality of high doctrine and of profound experience, and the privilege of Church membership, are all intended to fit them to walk worthily of their status as "Christ's men and women."

Christians as they tread the road of life and strive to be Christian in the fullest sense are confronted with four great imperatives, all of which are either explicit or implicit in Paul's description of personal Christian living as that occurs in the section of the Letter between Chapter IV, verse 17 and Chapter V, verse 20. The concrete ethical precepts which Paul sets forth in this passage group themselves under one or other of these great injunctions. Christians must "walk in the light." They must "copy God." They must "learn Christ." They must be "filled with the Spirit." All these imperatives flow directly from the truth of the Christian doctrine and the reality of the Christian experience with which Paul has dealt.

a) WALK IN THE LIGHT

This is the first great imperative of the Christian life. Christians are "children of light." They who were "once darkness and are now light in the Lord" (5:8) must become in daily living what they actually are by nature and status. Let the children of the Light express their true nature. Let them live in accordance with it. Let them show that they are not asleep, that they are wide awake, that for them the night is past, that life must be taken seriously and that eternity is now. They have been succoured by God from the realm of night. Let them now listen to God's demand that they live in His light.

This will mean for Christians a total break with their past. Formerly the great rift in their experience was a rift in their souls, a rift in their relationship with God. But now the great rift for them as Christians will be a total cleavage between the way they once lived and the way they must now live. They once lived "as the Gentiles do" (4:17). They must now live not as gentiles but as "saints," as "Christ's men and women." Why? Because the mass of mankind, the gentiles, those who do not know Jesus Christ, live a futile existence. They live "blindfolded in a world of illusion" (4:18). They are "cut off from the life of God through ignorance and insensitiveness" (4:18). The people whom they were once like, and whom they must still live among, "stifle their consciences and then surrender themselves to sensuality, practicing any form of impurity which lust can suggest." Moral purity, whereby men do not give rein to their lusts, but control them, is a primary desideratum of Christian living. To yield to bodily appetites, to indulge in sexual vice, to pamper the body or to be concerned about it as anything more than an instrument for what is spiritual, makes a person insensitive to moral obligations and darkens his insight into spiritual truth. No cultural ideal, no legalistic precept, no assent to an orthodox creed, no emotion stirred by the aesthetic accompaniments of religion, no enthusiasm for the institutional Church, can singly or together deal with the deep congenital problem of man's sinful nature. Only a new nature engendered by the Holy Spirit can solve the problem of man's propensity to evil.

Christians who have been delivered by Christ from serfdom to their own sinful nature will make it their supreme concern to know Christ's will for their lives (5:17). With an overwhelming sense of the value of time, and a clear discernment of the sinister forces that are at work in the world, they will live and act with all prudence, illumined by the light of truth.

But while a large part of Christian wisdom will be devoted to discerning and eschewing the wrong, the supreme task of Christians, as children of the Light, will be to allow the light of truth to illumine their minds in all their thinking and living. They will look at the whole life of man in the light of God and not in the light of what is purely sensate. They will see that the chief problems of human behavior and relationships grow out of the secularization of life, whereby men in their thinking and planning fail to take God and transcendent truth into account. They will see plainly that man's chief problem springs from his denial that there is any light other than the light of reason in which the human situation can be studied and its problems solved. But the "children of the Light" will know that there is not only a transcendent Light in which to regard the human situation, but that much of the light in which men study themselves and their world is, relatively speaking, pure darkness.

b) COPY GOD

This is the second great imperative (5:1). The life-long aspiration and task of Christians must be to be like God. It is important, of course, that they obey God; God's will must be their law; they must walk in His light. But that is not enough. They must strive earnestly to become like the God who commands them. Not only must their lives conform to His law; their nature must reflect His nature. In a word, they must bear God's image. They must show not only that they obey God but that they belong to God. They must show in their lives not only that they obey Him, but that they are like Him. Why? In a supreme sense, God's nature is the Christian's law. Because this is so, the end of all Christian living is to make God manifest, that is, to "glorify" God, to make Him visible to men.

The pursuit of God-likeness as the chief law and end of life stands in striking contrast to the pursuit of that false God-likeness which is the essence of sin. The devil, in Milton's *Paradise Lost*, wanted to be like God in order that he might be God's rival and owe nothing to God, not even gratitude. Those who follow this cue disown God; they throw off all allegiance to God and assume God's attributes in order to take God's place. They want to become gods in their own right. Quite different is that God-likeness which desires to be like God in order to glorify God, that is to say, in order that God may do His will and reveal His nature the more perfectly through the personality and activity of the human individual. To make God-likeness the goal of human behavior is greatly to simplify the whole ethical problem. The Christian can begin to clear from his head "masses of impressive rubbish" in the form of moral precepts. To copy God, to be "an imitator of God," is to be something much more than to be loyal to truth or even "loyal to loyalty." The ethical life takes on a new concreteness. It is to be like a Person, to reflect His image. Once again how true it is: Christian truth is personal truth throughout the whole range and implications of the meaning of truth.

The imperative to "copy God" has in the thinking of Paul some very important implications. It involves an expression of constant thankfulness to God. If Christians are to copy God and be like God, they must be thankful to God, both for what He is and for what He has done. For nothing keeps men closer to God than a sense of indebtedness to Him. Recognizing what God has done for him the Christian soul praises God. Praise to God is constantly enjoined in the Old Testament and in the New. He who "offers praise" as his sacrifice "glorifies" God, proclaims His true nature and the meaning of His deeds. God "inhabits," that is, is "enthroned upon" the "praises of Israel." God's true throne is the adoring worship of those who are overwhelmed by the splendor of His great plan to constitute a new order of being with Christ as its center. To identify oneself adoringly with this plan is the surest way for a Christian to become like God in thought and in life.

It is impossible, however, to copy God without realizing that in God's nature and in His divine activity there is an element of wrath. The wrath of God, as Paul puts it, "comes upon the children of disobedience." Men who try to thwart God, who establish and live by standards of behavior which violate God's nature and purpose, can have no real future in God's world. To imitate God means that there is a place in the Christian life for holy anger, that is to say, for an explicit reaction against every manifestation of human nature and every form of human activity which violate the supreme canon of human goodness as determined by the nature and activity of God. But let him who feels the stirring of anger in the presence of moral evil never try to take the place of God and administer justice. Vengeance belongs to God alone. In the mystery of our human existence and the complexities of moral behavior, we have often to tolerate evil. God, we are reminded by Jesus in another place, lets His rain come down on the evil as well as upon the good. It is only at the last, beyond history, following God's Judgment, that the influence of evil and of evil men will come to an end. To copy God, therefore, in the presence of evil may often mean a kind and tolerant attitude towards the human sinner, ever fleeing from self-righteousness, and recognizing that we, too, are sinners and must live by the mercy and forgiveness of God.

But beyond thankfulness for the goodness of God and acquiescence in the judgment of God, Christians must constantly endeavour to be conformed to the lowliness of God. To copy God has no meaning unless the Christian recognizes that the supreme fact about God is that He humbled Himself, that He continues to humble Himself, that He stoops to conquer. It is meet that Christians should copy the lowliness of God. Only when the soul is pierced with a sense of what God did for man, what He became for man, what He does for man, can true humility be created in the human soul. It is here that the great break takes place between the Christian ethic and every form of non-Christian ethical behavior. The Greek gentleman had no place for humility. The Stoic was proud that he could show himself superior to the bludgeonings of circumstance with "head bloody but unbowed."

In the classical tradition of the Hispanic world, the ideal of manhood was to feel that each Spaniard was a Caesar in his own native right. "Every Catalonian has a king within him," a famous motto ran. In the ethical tradition of paganism at its best, and in the ethical ideals of the Spanish nature which Christianity never tamed, there is no room for humility. The Spanish sense of honor, based upon a delirious sense of the grandeur of one's unconquered and unconquerable self, is the historical antithesis of that Christian humility which flows from the recognition of the fact that God humbled Himself.

We cannot grasp or feel the true majesty of the lowliness which Paul enjoins for wayfarers on the road of life without recalling the initial rapture with which he began to soar and sing, "Blessed be the God and Father of our Lord, Jesus Christ." To become blessed with the blessedness of God is to copy God in His lowliness, to become humanly great by the divine gentleness.

c) LEARN CHRIST

This leads us to the third imperative. This imperative is formulated by implication. By saying to the people to whom he wrote (4:20) that a certain type of behavior was contrary to everything that they had learned about Jesus Christ implied that for them to *learn Christ* was their great task.

The ultimate goal of human thought and behavior is to think and act "as the truth is in Jesus." The endeavor to "copy God" leads directly to Jesus Christ. To "learn Christ" is much more than to acquire knowledge about Him. It is to absorb Him and to be absorbed by Him. Christ the Personal Truth becomes the supreme copy, the standard image, which must be learned. And this lesson can only be learned when the Christ, who is Himself the lesson, becomes part of a Christian's very being, enlightening his mind, stirring his heart, controlling his will. When this takes place the Christian, to use Paul's other great category, which we will consider later, thinks and acts "in the Lord."

To learn Christ means, to begin with, to study carefully the life and teachings of Jesus. It means chiefly, however, to grasp the essential image of Jesus, which is the image of what God is and of what man should be, and, what through the grace of Jesus, he may become. That image, as has been emphasized already, was portrayed in the memorable foot-washing scene when the Master, intensely aware of His Deity and completely conscious of His destiny, became the servant. That image is projected by St. Paul in the Philippian Letter into the context and structure of the great cosmic drama. "Let this mind," he said, "be in you which was also in Christ Jesus, who, being in the form of God and thinking not equality with God a prize to be graspingly retained, humbled Himself and became obedient unto death, even the death of the cross" (Phil. 2:5–8). This is the tremendous thing for which Christians have to thank and praise God. This is also the image of what they, too, must become. Becoming themselves nothing that Christ may be all and in all in them and through them, they in their turn become all things to all men, the servants of all.

For a Christian to learn Christ in this sense is to put off his old nature, to repudiate everything in word and deed that "belongs to one's former manner of life and is corrupt through deceitful lusts" (Eph. 4:22). One becomes "renewed in the spirit of one's mind" (4:23). This happens because one has put on "the new nature created after the likeness of God in true righteousness and holiness" (4:24). Then God in Christ ceases to be a copy which is merely looked at. Christ in whom God comes to us, the image of the invisible God and the agent of His will, becomes our life, our true nature. Then goodness becomes not an imperative to be striven after but an activity in which we naturally engage. It becomes second nature.

They who have learned Christ put away every form of falsehood. They speak the truth to one another. They do this because lying is incompatible with the common life. A lie destroys the community. It shatters the basis of perfect trust upon which the Christian community is established. A lie is a stab into the very vitals of the Body of Christ. This is so because a lie is a sable shaft from the kingdom of darkness, and Christians must live in the light with perfect openness towards God and towards one another. There is no place in the Christian ethic for the well-intentioned lie. In the moral behavior which Christ inspires, the end never justifies the means. It is never legitimate, as the Grand Inquisitor [1] suggested it was, to tell people lies in their own interest. It is far better that people should know the truth. But the truth must always be told them in love. It must also be told them in the light of what God has done, is doing, and can do, so that those upon whose mind some terrible truth flashes may not be driven to despair (4:25).

Learning Christ is compatible with anger. Otherwise what meaning could it have for Christians that His eyes which oftentimes filled with tears flashed also with flame in the presence of people who exploited religion and dishonored the name of God. But if we are to learn Christ and copy God we must become angry without sinning. We must never allow ourselves so to think or act that our sinful self-will shall take the place of the will of God. Paul lays down this very human and timely injunction: "Let not the sun go down upon your wrath" (4:26), he says. That time in hours of darkness, when one is about to lay one's head in weariness upon one's pillow, is a bad time for anger to blaze forth. It is the worst possible time for a quarrel. No one is one's self when mind and body are exhausted and one is surrounded by the pall of darkness which is the symbol of evil and death. At the hour of retirement let one compose one's spirit, forgetting the wrongs one has received. With humble and trustful commitment of the whole case to God, let one take repose and await a new day to seek the solution of the vexed issue. Otherwise, the powers of darkness will find an inning and the devil will catch the human

---

[1] The Grand Inquisitor legend in Dostoievski's *The Brothers Karamazov*.

spirit off guard. Then the morning will break, not upon a Christian warrior ready to do justice, but upon a broken and dishonored man.

It is never right for a Christian to steal, to take what belongs to another. Let him meet his needs and the needs of others by honest toil. Christ knew what it meant to work with His hands. So did Paul who supported himself and his companions in their evangelistic labors by following his tent-making craft whenever the opportunity offered. True Christianity makes all work honorable. No one who is unwilling to work with his hands and to engage in honest toil, refusing to be a parasite and to live by the labors of others, living or dead, has ever learned Christ (4:28).

Neither has one learned Christ who maligns or vilifies people, who delights in proclaiming from the housetops their faults and foibles, luxuriating in gossip about the weaknesses of the saints. He has not learned Christ who in the name of truth and faithfulness unveils for unholy eyes the shortcomings of his friends. In the human spirit that has learned Christ there is no place for bitterness. Says Paul, "Let all bitterness and wrath and anger and clamor and slander be put away from you with all malice" (4:31). It is hard not to feel insulted and resentful when someone has said things about us, or done things to us, which affect our status or our prestige. The thing not to do is to allow the poison of hate to foul our inner life, to turn us into people with a "chip on our shoulders" or a perpetual grievance in our hearts which reflects itself in ceaseless peevishness, bitter imprecations, and hate. Woe betide the Christian who allows malice to breed within him a disposition to see in the worst light those who have wronged him and to harbor the malicious desire that they shall suffer. It is a terrible thing when life is guided and empowered by an uncontrollable vindictive passion to get one's man, to get even with him, and to cut one's pound of flesh from the part of him where it shall harm him most.

To learn Christ means this too. Instead of allowing ourselves to become mastered by all the powers of Hell, let us so learn Christ that our hearts shall be tender and our feelings kind. Let a disposition to forgive become regnant through the holy memory that we too were in desperate need of God's mercy and God in Christ forgave us. Therefore, says Paul, "Be kind one to another, tender hearted, forgiving one another as God in Christ forgave you" (4:32).

But if an inner disposition of affectionate kindness is to mark the life attitude of Christians, it is imperative that the Holy Spirit be given a chance. For it is the Holy Spirit alone who can create Christ-likeness in the soul. By the Holy Spirit Christians have been sealed with God's own mark to be His own possession. The gracious influence of the Holy Spirit makes it become more and more evident to whom Christians belong, what their ultimate loyalty is, what their affinities are. But the Holy Spirit is very sensitive. He can be grieved. According to Jesus Himself the sin against the Holy Ghost is to attribute to Satanic influence, traits and deeds of which the Spirit Himself is the author. It is also a sin against the Holy Ghost to allow one's self deliberately to yield to Satanic influences and dispositions in one's attitudes towards others. When one's vital force is thrown upon the side of evil and one refuses to be dictated to and guided by the Holy Spirit, the Spirit of God is grieved. When His gracious presence is withdrawn the horrors of Hell break out in Mansoul and the Diabolonians roam around at large. It was in view of that terrible possibility that Paul said, "And do not grieve the Holy Spirit of God by whom you were sealed unto the day of redemption" (4:30).

d) BE FILLED WITH THE SPIRIT

All the other imperatives have prepared us for this crowning injunction. We can walk in the light, we can copy God, we can learn Christ and give our uttermost allegiance to Him only if we are prepared to live a life of spiritual ardour. We come here to one of the paradoxes of the Christian religion in the sphere of ethical behaviour. Two things become compatible which are never found together outside that human spirit whom Jesus Christ has mastered. There is on the one hand deep calm, the peace of God which passes all understanding, a tender and kindly disposition even when one is wronged; there is present on the other hand, a deathless passion, an undying enthusiasm, elsewhere associated by Paul with the life of the athlete and of the soldier but which he here, in a very daring figure, associates with inebriation. The Christian who truly walks in the light, copies God, and learns Christ is an intoxicated being. But his inebriation is not caused by alcohol. It is no delicious delirium born of narcotics. It is a state of soul engendered by the Holy Spirit whereby the spirit of man is filled to capacity with the Spirit of God. "Do not get drunk with wine," says Paul, "for that is debauchery, but be filled with the Spirit" (5:18).

It is one of the tragedies of much orthodox Christian thinking, and still more of much sedate Christian living, that any suggestion of being Spirit-filled is associated with religious fanaticism or with the aberrations of sectarian groups that live upon the fringe of ecclesiastical Christianity. The place of emotion in human nature and in human living, very especially in the life and attitudes of Christians, needs to be rethought in our time. It is high time that we recognize that emotion is a constitutive part of human nature and must be given a legitimate expression in religion. We might go further and say that the expression of feeling is an essential aspect of the rational order of existence. Whether it be in the realm of scientific discovery or in the philosophical formulation of those assumptions which are called *a priori* truths of reason, nothing great ever takes place without emotion. Whether I say that matter or spirit is the ultimate reality, I am making an affirmation which has its source in feeling. It derives from the way in which I, in the course of my experience, have come to "feel" life. All great creative deeds are the fruit of passion in the purest sense. Nothing great has been ever accomplished in the secular or religious order except by souls aflame. It was not Unamuno, the interpreter of the spiritual ardour of the Spanish mystics and the disciple of Dostoievski and Kierkegaard, who said, "No soul is pure that is not passionate, no virtue is faith that is not enthusiastic." No, these were the words of a Christian Victorian, J. R. Seeley.[2]

And yet, of course, the danger inherent in emotional ardour is apparent. We have seen it in these last times in movements which are inspired by "truths gone mad." We have a right to fear the emergence, and still more the predominance, of fanaticism within the Christian community. And yet it is oftentimes very difficult to separate fanaticism from faith. We are constantly confronted with this dilemma. How shall we secure that everything be done "decently and in order" in the common life of the Christian community, while recognizing that fanaticism is of the lineage of faith? We would do well, in this connection, to listen to the wise words of Arnold J. Toynbee when, upon the basis of a profound study of human civilization, he bids us beware lest we "stifle fanaticism at the cost of extinguishing faith."

This is precisely the predicament in which contemporary Protestantism finds itself. We have frowned upon all manifestations of emotion. We have become fearful of chain reaction in the realm of feeling. We have convinced ourselves that the staid, conventional, honest, and kindly person who balks at the expression of any emotion which would express strong spiritual exaltation or depression, is the normal Christian type, whose genus we should universalize throughout the globe and hail as the true ecumenical Christian. The new vogue of dialectical thought, with its intense dislike of absolutes and its doctrine of synthetic compromise, tends to make Christians more and more wary of moods, attitudes, or slogans which appear to be extremist, the hallmark of people who feel that they have discovered the truth.

---

[2] Cf. *Ecce Homo*.

From time to time this neo-Hellenistic mood suffers a rude awakening. Our Christian Grecians are brought face to face with the fact that there are human situations so desperate, human beings so far down in sin or misery, so completely "lost," that they cannot be dealt with save by people of an emotional ardour whom conventional Christians despise. Yet those people are able to bring to bear upon their spiritual task an emotional approach so overwhelming that degraded human lives are transported out of the gutter in which they grovel and begin to conform to a highly spiritual pattern.

A number of years ago the writer of these lines was brought face to face with just this contingency. A leading Chilean educator, the head of one of Chile's leading institutions of higher learning and a man thoroughly acquainted with European and North American culture, affirmed once in my presence that, in his judgment, Protestantism was far too cold and far too exclusively concerned with ethics ever to reach the Chilean soul. "In the early days of our country's history," he said, "the Roman Catholic missionaries profoundly moved our people with the dazzling nature of their religious pageantry. That pageantry made an overwhelming impression upon multitudes of people who lived then, as they live now, on the perpetual brink of misery. It succeeded in transporting them inwardly above the sordid conditions of their daily life and gave them a feeling of importance. But you people," said he, "have nothing that can reach down to the soul depths of the Chilean masses." Since that time, however, an indigenous Pentecostal movement has broken out in Chile. In the intervening years the Christian community has been increased by several hundreds of thousands of people from the rural and industrial workers of the country. The movement, it is true, was accompanied at the beginning by strange phenomena, in the form of swoons and rhythmic dances and ecstatic utterances, which were characteristic of certain manifestations of the Christian religion in the first century. These phenomena, however, are gradually passing away. While not being suppressed, they are being discouraged by the religious leaders of this movement. Thousands of Chileans who were gripped in the depths of their souls by the story of the Cross of Christ and experienced the power of His Resurrection in the classical tradition of Christian evangelism now live the life of normal citizens. They do not lose their Christian zeal, but they have become interested in everything that concerns true manhood and womanhood and the tasks of good citizenship. What is more, they ardently desire to become related to fellow Christians. At the present moment the old Pentecostal Movement, once so disdained in more conventional Christian circles in Chile, is being regarded in those circles as a great spiritual achievement. On the other hand, government and civic authorities in Chilean society have come to regard the Movement as a great boon to the national life, and as a supreme contribution to the uplift of the masses and to public morals. I mention this because, when we deal in ecumenical circles with the problem of evangelism we cannot ignore movements of this kind. Such movements, no less than the fanatical devotees of political religion, have much to teach us in this hour. By studying these phenomena we may be able to recover and to reinterpret certain forgotten factors that are very basic to the Christian religion.

The secular religions of our time, which are Christianity's greatest rivals, have been marked by tremendous emotion which has derived directly from ideas. Communism is a singing faith, as was Nazism before it. Marxist Communists have a conviction that the "radiant forces of the universe" are on the side of their cause and that the Communist revolution is "what all time has willed." Chinese Communists have in these last years fought and sung and danced their way from Manchuria to the Siamese border, and from the Yalu River to the Thirty-eighth Parallel. Lenin's ideal for the Communist Party was that it should be a "militant monastic order." The Revolution needed followers who had the calm discipline of monks and the passionate ardour of crusaders.

But there is at the core of the Christian tradition, and very especially in the greatest of Christian documents which is the subject of this study, the pattern of a disciplined ardour, purer and stronger than any crusading devotion which the annals of history record. Christians "filled with the Spirit," with a holy inebriation, were "to address one another in psalms and hymns and spiritual songs, singing and making melody to the Lord with all their heart, and, always and for everything, giving thanks in the name of our Lord Jesus Christ to God the Father" (5:19, 20). The picture here given of Spirit-filled men and women, walking in the light, copying God, learning Christ, is that of brotherly enthusiasts. Enthusiasm and brotherliness, how difficult to find them together! And more difficult still, to hold them together! For enthusiasm tends to make people individualistic; they are so eager to forge ahead that they get out of step and break ranks. Their very ardour makes them subject to whims and they are natural enemies of the established, conventional order with its chilly proprieties. It is for that reason that in the course of the Church's history, ecclesiastics and enthusiasts have often been the human antitheses of one another. The official Church has often forced out of its membership individuals and groups regarded as unruly because they challenged established customs. "Glory to the Church and damnation to enthusiasts," was the motto engraven on a bell hung in the belfry of a new church in Cambridge, England, as a protest against the ministry of the famous university preacher, Charles Simeon. How can religious ardour be channelled? How can co-operation and unity be achieved between Christian enthusiasts and Christians of a more staid and conservative type? In a word, how can we wed ardour and order?

Before we commend the staid and condemn the passionate let us remember this. It is possible for Christian people to express brotherliness which moves towards, and which is consummated in, Church union, and still be devoid of redemptive ardour; for it is all too common for friendly relations and the absence of tensions and the joy of being together to become ends in themselves.

> For your friends are my friends, and my friends are your friends;
> And the more we get together, the happier we'll be.

When this ditty expresses the spirit of Christian togetherness, when Christians exult in unity and good fellowship just for their own sake, the Christian movement becomes sterile. The question arises: What is unity for; is it something merely to be extolled and enjoyed? Or is unity for something that lies beyond unity? For the Christian Church to be truly the Church, it is not enough that Christians express their love to God and to one another in corporate worship. The Church is truly the Church only when corporate worship, theological understanding and ecclesiastical unity move Christians to missionary ardour, inspiring them to move in crusading array beyond the portals of the sanctuary towards all the frontiers of the world.

The solution of this most difficult problem is for the Church to recover as a theological doctrine and as a spiritual reality, what Paul means by the Holy Spirit. For to the work of the Holy Spirit are attributed both spiritual ardour and spiritual order. Enthusiasm must be brotherly; brotherliness must be enthusiastic. Christian fraternity and missionary passion, both are needed and neither is complete without the other. Christians as *brotherly enthusiasts* are heirs of the great Biblical and classical tradition of their holy faith. They will not be alien at times to the rhapsodic ecstasy caused by a soaring vision or a glimpse into the heavenlies. The ideas they cherish and the experiences they enjoy and the high hopes of their calling will make them break forth into singing in "psalms and hymns and spiritual songs," blessing God the Father in the name of Jesus Christ His Son. Dedicated to do the will of God for the coming of the new divine order, theirs will be "a permanent intoxication of vital ardor." They will watch and wait, believing that the time draws near, that "the season's near its grain." Yet for all their ardour, or rather because of its enlightened and intensely spiritual character, they will live in the midst of the secular order and play their part in it; they will be relevant to their time and take their place in life's several spheres and vocations. Realizing that they have been baptized into one Spirit, they will work together and be patient with one another; aware that their warfare is not merely "with flesh and blood," they will arm themselves and keep themselves armed for spiritual combat.

We thus approach the end of the road. In the concluding part of this study we shall consider, under Paul's guidance, how "Christ's men and women" should act as members of the basic institutions of society, and how they should confront the "Principalities and Powers" which beset their pilgrim way.

CHAPTER IX

Christian Action on the Frontiers of Strife

Action, it has been said truly, is the essence of life, as combustion is the essence of flame. The concluding section of the Ephesian Letter is a call to action.

The redemptive purpose of God could be fulfilled only by action on His part. That same purpose demands action also on the part of those whose lives have been transformed by God's action and who have dedicated themselves to live for God's Order. What Paul has said thus far has inspired Christian mysticism, Christian theology, Christian liturgy, Christian poetry and fine arts, Christian ecclesiology, that is, discussion regarding the nature of the Church. But the divine purpose cannot be fulfilled, nor can Christians fulfill their true destiny, save in concrete action. God's order is such that men cannot think or feel or organize their way into it. Christians whose status and source of life in the heavenly sphere are in Christ must act "in the Lord" in the earthly sphere; and this each mature Christian must do as an individual person and not merely as a member of a mass society, secular or religious.

In calling men into citizenship in His new Order God individualizes. Those so called must act as individuals in the membership of that new Order. That they should so act is required both by the terms of God's purpose and by the demands of Christian maturity.

There are certain things in contemporary life which set in high relief the importance of the human individual and his personal action. The civilization of our time has been appropriately called a "sitting civilization." Those who travel at the greatest speed in the air or on the ground do so sitting in immobile posture, with no demand whatever upon physical effort. Physically and spiritually people prefer to sit. Why move? Why act? "Reach for the phone before you reach for your hat," said the advertisement of a telephone company in recent years. "Let him do anything but act," advises Screwtape in C. S. Lewis' profound and entertaining description of Satanic philosophy. And yet, as a keen psychologist has pointed out, "People generate fears when they sit and overcome them when they move." It is only in action that boredom can be overcome and the haunting fear of the next day be removed. How paradoxical it is that in military operations in these last times, despite the trend towards swift movement and complicated mechanization, the foot soldier is still crucial; he has in many instances been the sole master of the field. God requires that the citizens of His Kingdom should act, should walk, should fight, should ever move towards the frontiers where the crucial issues are. If they say "Lead on, O King Eternal," He will see to it that they "shall walk and not faint." "In the light" of an eternal purpose, "copying God," "learning Christ," "filled with the Spirit," the members of the Divine commonwealth shall enter into action.

In the final section of the Letter (5:22–6:24) we approach the frontier realities of life. Here Christians, as citizens of a new order, as members of the mystical Body of Christ, are required to act in the common life, in public and in private, as members of the human family, ever conscious that they may be subjected at any time to the assault of forces which they cannot control, and even of forces whose seat of power is the supernatural kingdom of evil.

The frontier sense, the sense of ever moving onward as pilgrims, ever ready to use one's weapons as soldiers, is deeply imbedded in the thought and imagery of the New Testament. In this concluding section of the Ephesian Letter we get the feel and the thrill of the essential frontiers of human existence. The Christian life cannot be lived in any private religious world. Christians can never become reconciled to a monastic or a ghetto existence. They cannot accept as ultimate any set of legal prescriptions imposed by ancient or modern Pharisees. Neither can they conform in their outlook and action to what men claim to be scientific truth. There is for them an everlasting beyond. In the geographical sphere they feel impelled, in loyalty to their Lord, and in response to God's great purpose which centers in Him, to carry the news of that purpose to all mankind. Paul himself had found, as a modern Jewish admirer has said of him, that "the Christ is a mighty hunter." "I followed Him," he said, "into strange cities." In the vocational sphere Christians must ever move beyond the spirit and standards which inspire thought and behaviour in all Life's natural orders and callings. In the specifically religious sphere they can never rest satisfied with a Church which worships God but does not bear witness to God. In their frontier life Christians are called upon to occupy and to evangelize all the unoccupied spaces in the inhabited globe and in the vocational life of mankind. They are also called upon to confront the whole hostile realm of "Principalities and Powers" who seek to thwart the coming of God's Order, the establishment of His Kingdom among men.

The "Frontiers," as we find them in the closing part of this Letter, are of two kinds. There are the *Frontiers of the Natural order* and there are the *Frontiers of the Supernatural order.*

a) THE FRONTIERS OF THE NATURAL ORDER

It is an impressive fact that Paul describes the Christian's approach to the two chief natural orders of man's life, the home and business.

In the home those live who are closest to a man by the ties of blood. The family relationship is not only the ultimate relationship, the first and basic relationship of human beings to one another. It has been consecrated by the Christian religion as a symbol of the relationship between God and men who are His children. Marriage, upon which the home is founded, has been made the emblem, or parable, of the relationship between Jesus Christ and His Church.

Man also must work; he must engage in business. "Man," says one of the great Psalms, "goeth forth to his work and to his labor until the evening" (Ps. 104:23). Between the morning, when a man leaves the home, and the evening when he returns to it, he is supposedly engaged in toil. He takes part in public affairs. He is a master or a servant. He belongs to management or to labor. He is a member of a social system in which he must play his part and earn his living, if he would support his home and further the interests of society.

Let us listen to Paul's words of counsel regarding the conduct of life in the domestic sphere and in public life.

The Principle of Christian Action: "In the Lord"

The supreme principle which is to guide Christians in all human relationships is "in the Lord," or "out of reverence for Christ" (Eph. 5:21). All things are to be done out of reverence for Him who is the supreme Master and Lord of every Christian soul. This normative principle derives, of course, from the more general basic imperative to "learn Christ." The presence of Christ in life, and the new nature or disposition which His presence gives to life, leads to the ethical principle of "reverence for Christ" as the norm or standard of Christian social behaviour. The Christ who becomes the object of reverence is, of course, both the Jesus of the Gospels and the Christ of the cosmic, redemptive drama. He is the Christ in whose eyes, at different times and in different circumstances, flashed the flame and glistened the tear. He is the Christ of the Descent and of the Ascent: the Christ of the Cross and of the Resurrection, the Christ of the Incarnation and of the Ascension. It is Jesus Christ in His fullness who is to be so reverenced that those who call themselves by His name shall act appropriately in His spirit. It might indeed be said that to act "out of reverence for Christ" and to act "in the Lord" are synonymous; for both imply the practical application to social relationships of what each Christian finds or should find in Jesus Christ.

Recognizing and applying this personalized standard, Christians should in every instance be "subject to one another," or rather "fit into one another." Though spiritually free and in Christ, "lords of all," they are, in Luther's words, to become also "servants of all." Only as Christians, in the spirit of Christ, prefer others to themselves, can there be brought into being that kind of articulation and harmony which a Christian society demands.

Action on the Domestic Frontier

Life in the home as the primary and basic institution of society comes in for special treatment. The home, by its very nature, should be the abode of love. The Christian home should, of course, fulfill everything that belongs inherently to domestic reality as an order of creation. The genius of the home is that every member of the family, being concerned about the interests and welfare of every other member and of the family as a whole, should act in a co-operative spirit. But the family, which is the first great frontier of human existence, can be a flaming frontier. It can be a frontier of violent conflict, and such it certainly has been, to a very large extent, since the dawn of human history. The most tragic conflicts, which have inspired tragic drama at its grimmest, have been conflicts in the domestic circle. One problem of the home is authoritarianism; the other is hedonism.

The authoritarian principle expresses itself when one member of the family, the father or the mother, or perchance, a sister or a brother, presumes to exercise absolute control in the family circle and to rule by pure force of one kind or another. The result is a doll house or a mad house. We have sepulchral quiet and orderliness imposed by fear; or we have chaotic disorder inspired by exasperation. In the one instance there is no spontaneity of behaviour, no initiative in action. In the other instance, there is nothing but frustration and neurosis. In either case the idea of the home and the reality of family life are destroyed.

The other bane of domestic bliss is hedonism. When a husband or a wife regards the marriage relationship and the founding of a family as an exclusive occasion for the securing of personal pleasure, the reality of marriage and of the home is destroyed. The exclusive egoistic cult of one's own happiness, the insistent demand for the satisfaction of what one regards as "vital" for one's own pleasure and well-being, is unworthy of a true husband or wife, and it can wreck a home. How often it happens that what a husband or a wife regards as "vital" to happiness becomes impossible of realization due to circumstances, it may be the health of the wife, or the business reverses of the husband. Tensions develop and a matrimonial rupture is threatened. If mutual sympathy and adjustment do not take account of changed circumstances, if a sense of responsibility does not triumph over a selfish craving for pleasure, a home may be destroyed. Frustration, incompatibility, cruelty, or worse may be alleged and a divorce secured. Then the filial image which sets forth God's relationship to men as the Heavenly Father, and the nuptial image which symbolizes the dramatic love of Jesus Christ for His Church, are both besmirched. Images which are the supreme expression of loving responsibility are rejected in the name of egoistic hedonism.

What guidance does Paul offer in such a situation? All the members of a home circle are in some way or another to consider the "Lord," "for the husband is the head of the wife as Christ is the head of the Church, His Body, and is Himself its Saviour" (Eph. 5:23). Husbands on their part are to "love their wives as Christ loved the Church and gave Himself for her" (5:25). Husbands should love their wives "as their own bodies." "He who loves his wife loves himself" (5:28). Husband and wife, like Christ and the Church, are indissolubly one. Children, on their part, should obey their parents *in the Lord*. Fathers, on their side, should not provoke or exasperate their children, but bring them up "in the discipline and instruction *of the Lord*" (Eph. 6:4).

What does this mean? The husband stands out as the head of the home. If he is to be head of the home, as Christ is head of the Church, then he must "learn Christ" and act "out of reverence for Christ"; for Christ always puts the interests of His Church beyond His own interests. He lived for the Church; He sought the perfection and welfare of the Church; He never bossed or bludgeoned the Church. Rather He wooed the Church and established His right to its reverence and obedience by His own pure worth. This is the secret and, is, so to speak, the law of the husband. Let his leadership become established by a process of wooing and of worth; let his will be accepted by the obvious wisdom of the advice he gives and the attitude he takes up with respect to his partner and to his children. As for the wife, let her, as far as possible, adapt herself to her husband, overlooking a multitude of his foibles and faults. Her love for him being taken for granted, let her seek to respect and reverence him, even when it may be difficult to do so. As regards the sons and daughters of the home, let them hold their parents in due honor simply because they are their parents; let them give them obedience *in the Lord*. But this possibility must also be contemplated. For children to obey their parents "in the Lord" can mean that, as they grow up and come to Christian maturity, they may not be able to accept their parents' point of view. Loyalty to Christ may lead them to do something contrary to their parents' will. This, however, is consonant with reverence for Christ. For there can be times when, for Christ's sake and in loyalty to His word and spirit, a son or a daughter may have to disobey their parents in order that they may be able to obey Christ. Thus the principle stands; the supreme law for domestic life is to think and act "in the Lord," and "out of reverence for Christ."

Action on the Business Frontier

The same principle holds true on the business frontier. The form of public life which is most common to all human beings is some vocation or sphere in which men engage in work to earn their living. As the home is supremely the sphere of love, business life, life on the farm, life in the office, life in the store, life in the factory, life in government should be the sphere of justice. Here too the prescribed principle for human relations centers concretely in "reverence for Christ."

Man must work. To be truly a man he must engage in honest, creative toil, whether to fulfill the necessities of his own manhood as a person, or to earn a livelihood for those to whom he is bound by family ties, or to render a service to society. Even in primitive forms of human society, the relationship exists between master and servant, between management and labor. In modern society all social relations that involve work are directly related to, or live in the shadow or atmosphere of, industrialization. The machine, with its consequent mechanization and mass production, has radically changed both the nature and the problems of the master-servant relationship.

In exploring the bearing of the Christian principle of "reverence for Christ" upon the complexities of modern industrialized society certain things should be borne in mind. From the beginning of the Christian religion Christians and the Christian Church have had to live in many diverse forms of human society. They have had to bear their witness under very different forms of government. No form of organized society can be regarded by the Christian as absolutely and in every respect ideal, that is, as having an absolute divine sanction. There is no form of social organization which can be regarded as so authoritative and inspired that it can be equated with the Kingdom of God. The principle that "order is order" is as true in secular society as we have held it to be true in the organized structure of the Christian Church. There are authoritative Christian principles for the organization of society and for the conduct of social relationships. But there are no specific authoritative patterns for the detailed operation of social life or business relationships. All that can be said is that a truly democratic society, in which responsible principles of human behaviour and the dignity and rights of human beings are duly recognized, is the best and most desirable form of social organization which history has yet known. Yet, neither democracy nor any other form of social organization can, as I have said, be identified with the Kingdom of God. Only when God's Kingdom comes and the principles of "reverence for Christ" as the full manifestation of the righteousness and love of God becomes regnant, shall mankind acclaim the ideal society. In the meantime, laying aside all utopianism and not engaging in apocalyptic dreams, let us explore the principle of "reverence for Christ" amid the concrete realities of the labor situation in the society which we know.

An industrialized society, which technology has made possible, confronts two great perils both of which must be described and examined "in the Lord." One of these perils is the *depersonalization of the workman;* the other is the *tyrannization of the master.*

In the particular conditions under which men work today millions of human beings are simply caught in a wheel. They are just so many hands that toil, they are just tools that function, they are human ciphers whose existence is tabulated by a counting machine. In such conditions human beings tend to lose their individuality; the traces of God's image in man which every man bears and should cultivate in creative work and the cultivation of personal interests, tend to disappear.

From the side of the master the peril is tyrannization. In these last times the master can become the state, divorced entirely from the desires and interests of the citizen. Totalitarian tyranny in which society and the state become merged, and technology which enables an oligarchy to achieve supreme and unchallenged power, make possible and have made actual the most acute form of tyrannization which history has ever known. Government becomes the absolute master of human life, citizens lose their freedom and become serfs.

What guidance does Paul offer for such a situation? The Christian workman is to take his work as seriously as he takes his Lord. If his work is real work then it is work to be done. It is work which is worthy of his best, work in which he should take personal pride. For the work's sake let him forget his masters, even though they be unjust and tyrannical. Let him work with the same singleness of heart as if he were working for Jesus Christ Himself. Let his criterion be not whether he is being watched, or whether his work is going to please men or not. As a servant of Christ, let him do his very best. In so doing, let him have the assurance that Christ will reward him for his toil. As a man under superior orders, serving a Lord who has given him a pattern of good workmanship, let him put his best endeavours into every moment of working time. Whatever be his quarrel with the conditions under which his work has to be carried on, let the fruit of his toil bear the stamp of his ideal. This does not mean, however, that as a man, as a citizen, and as a Christian, a workman should not strive for better working conditions. But let not his struggle for justice interfere with the quality of his service. He has a right to complain; he has no right to do an inferior job. He has a right to strike, but not to engage in sabotage. Under certain circumstances he has a right to be a revolutionary. He should even become a revolutionary, in the interests of men who suffer, when his masters govern in such a way as to run counter to God's moral order. But no revolutionary activity, let me repeat, can ever justify the breach of responsibility to do good work when one has a task to perform.

As regards the master, whether he be a man or a social or political system, if so be that the name of Christ is known and honored by him or by it, let the dignity of every human workman be recognized. Let men be stimulated to work by positive inducements to superior labor and not be threats if they fail. Let every system of power which acknowledges the place of Christ in human life proceed with justice and impartiality. Let it be remembered that Christ is no snob. He has no preference whatever for people who have more power or wealth than others, or who think themselves to be natively superior to others. For Him the servant is as good as the master, and He will exercise right judgment. But where the master or the power system neither knows nor acknowledges Christ both will be brought into judgment by Christ. Let tyranny tremble; let tyrants "kiss the son," for God, as Paul once said to the philosophers who came together on the Athenian Areopagus, "will judge the world in righteousness by a man whom he has appointed" (Acts 17:31).

It is plain that in all matters relating to life on the flaming frontiers of the natural order Christian laymen and laywomen occupy a place of special responsibility. They have a very special function to perform. The increasing sophistication of thought and the advancing secularization of life give to the men and women who live in closest contact with the realities of the secular order a deeper insight into the human problem than that which is ordinarily possessed by the clergy. For the same reason the laity, when they take seriously the great Christian principles of reverence for Christ, have strategic opportunities for introducing Christian solutions into private and public life. Today is the great era of the Christian layman.

b) THE FRONTIERS OF THE SUPERNATURAL ORDER

Paul began this Letter by a rhapsodical flight into the heavenly sphere. There he explored all that it meant by the affirmation that God has blessed Christians "with all spiritual blessing in Christ." He ends his Letter with a sober, realistic description of the terrestrial sphere where Christians must stand and fight. But this struggle on the roads of earth Christians will carry on in the power of their celestial Lord. They will have to fight, however, against the spiritual forces hostile to man's welfare which have their seat beyond earth and above history. Christians, says Paul, are not up against any merely physical enemy. They are up against "organizations and powers that are spiritual." Above all, they are up against "the unseen Power that controls this dark world, and spiritual agents from the very headquarters of evil" (6:12) (Phillips translation).

Paul, like Jesus, had an intense awareness of the personal character of the powers of evil in the universe. He recognized an organized strategy of evil. Here is something quite different from the power of heredity, something more grim and awesome than those judicial, dialectical forces which operate in history, whereby at times history fools man's logic and at other times brings to destruction his titanic pride. Paul was thinking of forces quite distinct from those demonic powers in contemporary history which arrogate to themselves the status and attributes of Deity, those powers which endeavour to control history as if there was no God and no eternal purpose running through and working itself out in the ages. While Paul, if he were living today, would take full cognizance of all those forces before which ordinary men in these times find themselves so helpless, he would still insist upon the personal character of supernatural evil. He would insist upon the reality of "the world rulers of this present darkness, the spiritual hosts of wickedness in the heavenly places" (6:12). He asks, therefore, the men and women to whom he wrote to find their strength "not in yourselves but in the Lord, in the power of his boundless resource." "Put on God's complete armor," he says to them, "so that you can successfully resist all the devil's methods of attack." "You must wear," he goes on, "the whole armor of God that you may be able to resist evil in its day of power, and that even when you have fought to a standstill you may still stand your ground" (Phillips translation).

It is important to observe at this point something of great spiritual significance. Paul began his Letter by talking to individual Christians as such; he makes clear at its close that it is not en masse that Christians must fight the devil, but as individuals. In the context of the cosmic struggle between good and evil, between God and Satan, every victory of each individual Christian is a defeat for the cosmic powers of evil. We who are accustomed to regard victory solely in terms of organizational movements and their success, would do well to remember this. A victory over temptation won by the most insignificant Christian soul has a cosmic dimension. It breaks part of the power of the Enemy and brings the Kingdom of God nearer. More ultimate even than the organized Church of Christ on earth is the individual soul. Souls, which in the words of the great historian, are more important than civilizations, have in certain periods of history been more important also than organized Churches. Such souls, belonging to Christ and being members of His Mystical Body, may exercise on occasion enormous spiritual influence, though they may be compelled to live a solitary existence and be unrecognized and unrequited by the organized Church of Christ.

The Panoply of God

Empowered "in the Lord," Christians will wage a successful warfare if they arm themselves with the armor, and make use of the weapons, which God Himself provides for the great conflict. The pieces of armour are, as it happens, seven in number, suggestive of spiritual completeness. It is clear, however, that no attempt is made to describe the full panoply of a Roman legionary. Lacking, for example, are the greaves and the pike. When the pieces are analyzed it is evident that they fall into two groups: minor pieces and major pieces.

First and most crucial among the *minor* pieces is the *breastplate of righteousness*. The breastplate protects the heart. A Christian cannot engage in successful spiritual struggle unless he possesses personal integrity. His record must be clear. He must be above reproach. There must be in him no secret sin which has been unconfessed. He must be no hypocrite, that is, a play-actor who wears a mask, and who appears to other folk as a person very different from what he actually is. Freely admitting his sinfulness and his personal unworthiness, the life of the Christian warrior will be open towards God and man. He will possess that inward purity which comes from "willing one thing." Such pride as he may have will not be in his own achievements, nor in any personal graces, but solely in his scars, the "marks of the Lord Jesus," which have come to him in his struggle for righteousness.

Next in importance among the minor pieces is the *shield of faith*. A Christian's trust must be in God. He must cherish no doubt regarding the basis of his faith and the truth of his cause. He must be a man of intense conviction who has about him that air of calm decision which marks the man whose mind is resolute, whose bed is made. He knows who he is and to whom he belongs. There are many things about Christ and his own life and the purposes of God which he does not know, but there are some things, the basic things, which he does know; and he will stand ready at any time, if a person asks him, to give a reason for his hope. With his shield of faith he will be able to parry and neutralize the force of any gibes or insinuations, sneers or aspersions, doubts or threats, that may be hurled at him.

Upon the head of the spiritual crusader is the *helmet of salvation*. Wearing this helmet he can hold his head erect as a soldier fighting for the Kingdom of God, one who knows that Jesus

Christ is Lord, and that the decisive battle of the great campaign has been already won. He knows that Christ, in His life and death and by His glorious resurrection, defeated "Principalities and Powers" and "made a show of them openly, triumphing over them in His Cross." He can, therefore, look his enemies in the face. He knows that all Christ's foes and his are doomed, and that the eternal purpose of God in Christ shall be fulfilled in history and beyond history. Of this, too, he is fully aware: In the great campaign for the Kingdom no more than skirmishes and mopping up operations remain. Then at the last, as Paul wrote in another prison letter, his letter to the Philippians, "every tongue shall confess that Jesus Christ is Lord to the glory of God the Father" (Phil. 2:11).

Now the four major pieces:

Basic and indispensable for the Christian warrior, whom Paul describes in terms of a Roman legionary, is the *girdle* or *belt*. By the belt he is girded for action. At the close of a period of relaxation, and at the trumpet's call, the legionary donned his armour and tightened his belt. Without such girding he would be loosely hung together. With it he was ready and braced up. So Paul said, "Tighten the belt of truth about your loins" (Eph. 6:14). Truth here means absolute sincerity, downright, whole-hearted, unreserved devotion to the cause in which and for which one became a soldier. A Christian warrior who has tightened around him the belt of truth does not set out on an excursion in search of truth as if it were a lovely butterfly or an elusive bird. Such excursions have their very real place in life. They may even engage the legionary in his off-times of leisure. But his main task is of a sterner kind. Truth is something from which he starts and not something which he delights to chase. Truth, in the most basic sense, must be the possession of a Christian's life and not the pursuit of his leisure. And yet, in the last analysis, Truth is not something which the Christian has at all, whether as badge or adornment, whether as a banner which he unfurls, a torch which he flames into the darkness, or as a beacon which illumines the night. It is all that, but it is much more. It is something which has him, which possesses and engirdles him. It is a belt drawn tight around his loins. It is a loving and almighty Arm.

Then come the warrior's *shoes* with which his crusading feet are shod. Without proper footwear real campaigning is impossible. With the right shoes the soldier has complete mobility of movement. Campaign shoes are for all soils and seasons. Rightly shod the campaigner can adapt himself to all circumstances. He can tread meadow paths that lie by still waters; he can trudge over jagged rocks and climb the mountain trails. The Christian warrior's shoes are the stability of the "Gospel of peace." There are no shoes like these. They make a man run or walk with greater swiftness and more staying power than did the shoes of any of the fabled figures of legend. "How beautiful upon the mountains are the feet of him that bringeth good tidings." Equipped with the "Good News" the Christian feels an urge to go everywhere with the message—to walk all over "God's earth."

In the warrior's hand is a *sword*. It serves him for self-defense and to carry the offensive into enemy territory. It is "the Sword of the Spirit, the Word of God." Jesus when assaulted by Satan used it to thwart the Tempter's wiles. The Word of God, as Bunyan's pilgrim found, is "a right Jerusalem blade." In the hands of each Christian "Greatheart" it has a cutting edge. Its gleam in the darkness of the present illumines the ages. Its sharpness divides things up that do not naturally belong together. It probes to the core of human issues. It cuts Gordian knots and rips away the masks of falsehood. Armed with the Sword of the Spirit, the Christian hues his way through a tangle of circumstance. Concerned only with what the Lord God has said and would have him speak, he stands his ground undismayed and pursues the foe into his own territory.

Most potent weapon of all, that in which the seven pieces of the Christian armour culminate, is a weapon called *"all prayer."*

To wield this weapon is to pray at all times in the Spirit. Let the crusader allow the indwelling Holy Spirit to make intercession within him, with agonizing groans, and true knowledge of the will of God. Let him use every kind of prayer—at times a simple ejaculation for help, at times the prayer of quiet communion. Let him persevere in prayer, being alert and insistent in it, praying without ceasing. And let him pray for all "Christ's men and women," for individuals within the Church and for the Church as a whole throughout the inhabited earth.

EPILOGUE

Courage, Therefore!

The Letter closes with a personal plea. In their prayers let not the members of Christ's great Church Universal, to whom this ecumenical letter is sent, forget its author, Christ's ambassador, in his Roman prison. For it was in a prison cell that Paul had his double vision of God's heavenly counsel and of the Church's earthly pilgrimage. For him, Christ's prisoner, let their prayers ascend that as an "ambassador in chains" he might to his last breath make known to all and sundry God's unveiled secret in Jesus Christ through the Gospel. As regards all else, his faithful friend and Christian brother, Tychicus, would let them know personally how it fared with him. He would be the bearer of the Letter.

In their Christian warfare, amid all their struggles for the faith, let peace be theirs, peace in the midst of battle. And let them experience "love with faith, from God the Father and the Lord Jesus Christ." Paul's final desire was that they and everyone everywhere, who sincerely loved this Lord Jesus Christ, with an undying, sincere and imperishable love, should be objects of that holy transforming influence, that enabling power which is grace, the grace of God. By grace they had been saved; by grace they must be kept.

Not long after the Ephesian Letter had been written and read Christ's "ambassador in chains" gave his last witness to the Gospel before the Emperor. Centuries later when Rome was falling and another Caesar, the Emperor Justinian, was betaking himself to flight, his wife refused to leave the doomed city, and gave utterance to the famous saying, "Empire is a fine winding sheet."

Inspired by an imperial vision, Paul wrote of the United Kingdom of Earth and Heaven when the Roman Empire was at the height of its glory. Then when his fight was over and his course was run, and his fate as a martyr had been determined, he wrapt himself in the winding sheet of the Kingdom of God. In the great Christian tradition of dying in order to live, Paul sowed himself as a seed in the furrow of a doomed city, in the sure hope that what he had said and stood for would produce, at the last, a harvest of righteousness in the City of God which was destined to rise upon its ruins.

Appendix

THE LETTER OF PAUL TO THE EPHESIANS

1 Paul, an apostle of Christ Jesus by the will of God,
To the saints who are also faithful in Christ Jesus:
2 Grace to you and peace from God our Father and the Lord Jesus Christ.

3 Blessed be the God and Father of our Lord Jesus Christ, who has blessed us in Christ with every spiritual blessing in the heavenly places, 4 even as he chose us in him before the foundation of the world, that we should be holy and blameless before him. 5 He destined us in love to be his sons through Jesus Christ, according to the purpose of his will, 6 to the praise of his glorious grace which he freely bestowed on us in the Beloved. 7 In him we have redemption through his blood, the forgiveness of our trespasses, according to the riches of his grace 8 which he lavished upon us. 9 For he has made known to us in all wisdom and insight the mystery of his will, according to his purpose which he set forth in Christ 10 as a plan for the fullness of time, to unite all things in him, things in heaven and things on earth.

11 In him, according to the purpose of him who accomplishes all things according to the counsel of his will, 12 we who first hoped in Christ have been destined and appointed to live for the praise of his glory. 13 In him you also, who have heard the word of truth, the gospel of your salvation, and have believed in him, were sealed with the promised Holy Spirit, 14 which is the guarantee of our inheritance until we acquire possession of it, to the praise of his glory.

15 For this reason, because I have heard of your faith in the Lord Jesus and your love toward all the saints, 16 I do not cease to give thanks

---

The text of *The Letter of Paul to the Ephesians* is from the *Revised Standard Version of the Bible*, copyrighted 1952, by the Division of Christian Education, National Council of Churches, and used by permission.

for you, remembering you in my prayers, [17] that the God of our Lord Jesus Christ, the Father of glory, may give you a spirit of wisdom and of revelation in the knowledge of him, [18] having the eyes of your hearts enlightened, that you may know what is the hope to which he has called you, what are the riches of his glorious inheritance in the saints, [19] and what is the immeasurable greatness of his power in us who believe, according to the working of his great might [20] which he accomplished in Christ when he raised him from the dead and made him sit at his right hand in the heavenly places, [21] far above all rule and authority and power and dominion, and above every name that is named, not only in this age but also in that which is to come; [22] and he has put all things under his feet and has made him the head over all things for the church, [23] which is his body, the fullness of him who fills all in all.

2 And you he made alive, when you were dead through the trespasses and sins [2] in which you once walked, following the course of this world, following the prince of the power of the air, the spirit that is now at work in the sons of disobedience. [3] Among these we all once lived in the passions of our flesh, following the desires of body and mind, and so we were by nature children of wrath, like the rest of mankind. [4] But God, who is rich in mercy, out of the great love with which he loved us, [5] even when we were dead through our trespasses, made us alive together with Christ (by grace you have been saved), [6] and raised us up with him, and made us sit with him in the heavenly places in Christ Jesus, [7] that in the coming ages he might show the immeasurable riches of his grace in kindness toward us in Christ Jesus. [8] For by grace you have been saved through faith; and this is not your own doing, it is the gift of God—[9] not because of works, lest any man should boast. [10] For we are his workmanship, created in Christ Jesus for good works, which God prepared beforehand, that we should walk in them.

[11] Therefore remember that at one time you Gentiles in the flesh, called the uncircumcision by what is called the circumcision, which is made in the flesh by hands—[12] remember that you were at that time separated from Christ, alienated from the commonwealth of Israel, and strangers to the covenants of promise, having no hope and without God in the world. [13] But now in Christ Jesus you who once were far off have been brought near in the blood of Christ. [14] For he is our peace, who has made us both one, and has broken down the dividing wall of

hostility, [15] by abolishing in his flesh the law of commandments and ordinances, that he might create in himself one new man in place of the two, so making peace, [16] and might reconcile us both to God in one body through the cross, thereby bringing the hostility to an end. [17] And he came and preached peace to you who were far off and peace to those who were near; [18] for through him we both have access in one Spirit to the Father. [19] So then you are no longer strangers and sojourners, but you are fellow citizens with the saints and members of the household of God, [20] built upon the foundation of the apostles and prophets, Christ Jesus himself being the chief cornerstone, [21] in whom the whole structure is joined together and grows into a holy temple in the Lord; [22] in whom you also are built into it for a dwelling place of God in the Spirit.

3 For this reason I Paul, a prisoner for Christ Jesus on behalf of you Gentiles—[2] assuming that you have heard of the stewardship of God's grace that was given to me for you, [3] how the mystery was made known to me by revelation, as I have written briefly. [4] When you read this you can perceive my insight into the mystery of Christ, [5] which was not made known to the sons of men in other generations as it has now been revealed to his holy apostles and prophets by the Spirit; [6] that is, how the Gentiles are fellow heirs, members of the same body, and partakers of the promise in Christ Jesus through the gospel.

[7] Of this gospel I was made a minister according to the gift of God's grace which was given me by the working of his power. [8] To me, though I am the very least of all the saints, this grace was given, to preach to the Gentiles the unsearchable riches of Christ, [9] and to make all men see what is the plan of the mystery hidden for ages in God who created all things; [10] that through the church the manifold wisdom of God might now be made known to the principalities and powers in the heavenly places. [11] This was according to the eternal purpose which he has realized in Christ Jesus our Lord, [12] in whom we have boldness and confidence of access through our faith in him. [13] So I ask you not to lose heart over what I am suffering for you, which is your glory.

[14] For this reason I bow my knees before the Father, [15] from whom every family in heaven and on earth is named, [16] that according to the riches of his glory he may grant you to be strengthened with might through his Spirit in the inner man, [17] and that Christ may dwell in your hearts through faith; that you, being rooted and grounded in love,

[18] may have power to comprehend with all the saints what is the breadth and length and height and depth, [19] and to know the love of Christ which surpasses knowledge, that you may be filled with all the fullness of God.

[20] Now to him who by the power at work within us is able to do far more abundantly than all that we ask or think, [21] to him be glory in the church and in Christ Jesus to all generations, for ever and ever. Amen.

4 [1] I therefore, a prisoner for the Lord, beg you to lead a life worthy of the calling to which you have been called, [2] with all lowliness and meekness, with patience, forbearing one another in love, [3] eager to maintain the unity of the Spirit in the bond of peace. [4] There is one body and one Spirit, just as you were called to the one hope that belongs to your call, [5] one Lord, one faith, one baptism, [6] one God and Father of us all, who is above all and through all and in all. [7] But grace was given to each of us according to the measure of Christ's gift. [8] Therefore it is said,

"When he ascended on high he led a host of captives, and he gave gifts to men."

[9] (In saying, "He ascended," what does it mean but that he had also descended into the lower parts of the earth? [10] He who descended is he who also ascended far above all the heavens, that he might fill all things.) [11] And his gifts were that some should be apostles, some prophets, some evangelists, some pastors and teachers, [12] for the equipment of the saints, for the work of ministry, for building up the body of Christ, [13] until we all attain to the unity of the faith and of the knowledge of the Son of God, to mature manhood, to the measure of the stature of the fullness of Christ; [14] so that we may no longer be children, tossed to and fro and carried about with every wind of doctrine, by the cunning of men, by their craftiness in deceitful wiles. [15] Rather, speaking the truth in love, we are to grow up in every way into him who is the head, into Christ, [16] from whom the whole body, joined and knit together by every joint with which it is supplied, when each part is working properly, makes bodily growth and upbuilds itself in love.

[17] Now this I affirm and testify in the Lord, that you must no longer live as the Gentiles do, in the futility of their minds; [18] they are darkened in their understanding, alienated from the life of God because of

the ignorance that is in them, due to their hardness of heart; [19] they have become callous and have given themselves up to licentiousness, greedy to practice every kind of uncleanness. [20] You did not so learn Christ!—[21] assuming that you have heard about him and were taught in him, as the truth is in Jesus. [22] Put off your old nature which belongs to your former manner of life and is corrupt through deceitful lusts, [23] and be renewed in the spirit of your minds, [24] and put on the new nature, created after the likeness of God in true righteousness and holiness.

[25] Therefore, putting away falsehood, let every one speak the truth with his neighbor, for we are members one of another. [26] Be angry but do not sin; do not let the sun go down on your anger, [27] and give no opportunity to the devil. [28] Let the thief no longer steal, but rather let him labor, doing honest work with his hands, so that he may be able to give to those in need. [29] Let no evil talk come out of your mouths, but only such as is good for edifying, as fits the occasion, that it may impart grace to those who hear. [30] And do not grieve the Holy Spirit of God, in whom you were sealed for the day of redemption. [31] Let all bitterness and wrath and anger and clamor and slander be put away from you, with all malice, [32] and be kind to one another, tenderhearted, forgiving one another, as God in Christ forgave you.

5 Therefore be imitators of God, as beloved children. [2] And walk in love, as Christ loved us and gave himself up for us, a fragrant offering and a sacrifice to God.

[3] But immorality and all impurity or covetousness must not even be named among you, as is fitting among saints. [4] Let there be no filthiness, nor silly talk, nor levity, which are not fitting; but instead let there be thanksgiving. [5] Be sure of this, that no immoral or impure man, or one who is covetous (that is, an idolater), has any inheritance in the kingdom of Christ and of God. [6] Let no one deceive you with empty words, for it is because of these things that the wrath of God comes upon the sons of disobedience. [7] Therefore do not associate with them, [8] for once you were darkness, but now you are light in the Lord; walk as children of light [9] (for the fruit of light is found in all that is good and right and true), [10] and try to learn what is pleasing to the Lord. [11] "Take no part in the unfruitful works of darkness, but instead expose them. [12] For it is a shame even to speak of the things that they do in secret; [13] but

when anything is exposed by the light it becomes visible, for anything that becomes visible is light. [14] Therefore it is said,

> "Awake, O sleeper, and arise from the dead, and Christ shall give you light."

[15] Look carefully then how you walk, not as unwise men but as wise, [16] making the most of the time, because the days are evil. [17] Therefore do not be foolish, but understand what the will of the Lord is. [18] And do not get drunk with wine, for that is debauchery; but be filled with the Spirit, [19] addressing one another in psalms and hymns and spiritual songs, singing and making melody to the Lord with all your heart, [20] always and for everything give thanks in the name of our Lord Jesus Christ to God the Father.

[21] Be subject to one another out of reverence for Christ. [22] Wives, be subject to your husbands, as to the Lord. [23] For the husband is the head of the wife as Christ is the head of the church, his body, and is himself its Savior. [24] As the church is subject to Christ, so let wives also be subject in everything to their husbands. [25] Husbands, love your wives, as Christ loved the church and gave himself up for her, [26] that he might consecrate her, having cleansed her by the washing of water with the word, [27] that the church might be presented before him in splendor, without spot or wrinkle or any such thing, that she might be holy and without blemish. [28] Even so husbands should love their wives as their own bodies. He who loves his wife loves himself. [29] For no man ever hates his own flesh, but nourishes and cherishes it, as Christ does the church, [30] because we are members of his body. [31] "For this reason a man shall leave his father and mother and be joined to his wife, and the two shall become one." [32] This is a great mystery, and I take it to mean Christ and the church; [33] however, let each one of you love his wife as himself, and let the wife see that she respects her husband.

6 Children, obey your parents in the Lord, for this is right. [2] "Honor your father and mother" (this is the first commandment with a promise), [3] "that it may be well with you and that you may live long on the earth." [4] Fathers, do not provoke your children to anger, but bring them up in the discipline and instruction of the Lord.

[5] Slaves, be obedient to those who are your earthly masters, with fear and trembling, in singleness of heart, as to Christ; [6] not in the way of eyeservice, as men-pleasers, but as servants of Christ, doing the will

of God from the heart, ⁷ rendering service with a good will as to the Lord and not to men, ⁸ knowing that whatever good any one does, he will receive the same again from the Lord, whether he is a slave or free. ⁹ Masters, do the same to them, and forbear threatening, knowing that he who is both their Master and yours is in heaven, and that there is no partiality with him.

10 Finally, be strong in the Lord and in the strength of his might. ¹¹ Put on the whole armor of God, that you may be able to stand against the wiles of the devil. ¹² For we are not contending against flesh and blood, but against the principalities, against the powers, against the world rulers of this present darkness, against the spiritual hosts of wickedness in the heavenly places. ¹³ Therefore take the whole armor of God, that you may be able to withstand in the evil day, and having done all, to stand. ¹⁴ Stand therefore, having girded your loins with truth, and having put on the breastplate of righteousness, ¹⁵ and having shod your feet with the equipment of the gospel of peace; ¹⁶ above all taking the shield of faith, with which you can quench all the flaming darts of the evil one. ¹⁷ And take the helmet of salvation, and the sword of the Spirit, which is the word of God. ¹⁸ Pray at all times in the Spirit, with all prayer and supplication. To that end keep alert with all perseverance, making supplication for all the saints, ¹⁹ and also for me, that utterance may be given me in opening my mouth boldly to proclaim the mystery of the gospel, ²⁰ for which I am an ambassador in chains; that I may declare it boldly, as I ought to speak.

21 Now that you also may know how I am and what I am doing, Tych'ı-cus the beloved brother and faithful minister in the Lord will tell you everything. ²² I have sent him to you for this very purpose, that you may know how we are, and that he may encourage your hearts.

23 Peace be to the brethren, and love with faith, from God the Father and the Lord Jesus Christ. ²⁴ Grace be with all who love our Lord Jesus Christ with love undying.

INDEX

Aberdeen, 8
Abraham, 40, 55-56, 69-70, 72, 79, 108
Adam, 81, 124
Adam, The Second, 81
Agape, 64, 103
À Kempis, Thomas, 5
Anonymity, 41-42, 102
Antioch, 125
Apocalypse, The, 2, 84, 146
Apostles, 145-146, 149
Apostles' Creed, The, 83, 92
Apostolic Age, The, 4, 138
Apostolic Proclamation, The, 2
Aristotle, 55
Atonement, The, 84-87, 93
Auden, W. H., 21, 55, 77, 111
Augustine, 38
Augustus, 47, 76
Authoritarianism, 189
Authority, Biblical, 4ff.

Baal, 107
Babylonia, 70, 101
Bach, J. S., 24
Banality, 41-42
Baptism, 139, 141-143, 163
Bargaining, The Way of, 107
Barmen, 95
Barth, Karl, 68, 127, 143
Baudelaire, P. C., 29
Bethlehem, 21, 77
Biblical Authority, 4ff.
Blake, William, 2-3, 23, 100

Boehme, Jacob, 30
Brotherhood, 143-144, 181-182
Brothers Karamazov, The, 174
Brown, Baldwin, 13
Buddha, Buddhism, 47, 76, 103
Bunyan, John, 19, 104, 113, 116, 199

Calvin, John, 67, 148, 157
Carlyle, Thomas, 118
Catholicity, Evangelical, 162
Chalmers, Thomas, 118-119, 120-121
Charity, Theological, 152
Chile, 179-180
Christ of Velásquez, The, 91
Christian Life, The True, 167ff.
Christian Witness in Everyday Life, 184ff.
Christmas Oratorio, A, 21, 111
Church, The
  Body of Christ, The, 61, 69, 71, 94, 97, 117-118, 122-126, 128, 134-136, 140, 149-151, 154, 158, 160-163, 166, 174, 185, 190, 196
  Building, The, 130-132
  Bride of Christ, The, 130, 132-134, 167
Church, Eastern Orthodox, 128, 156
Church, Roman Catholic, 48, 102, 107-109, 128, 131, 133, 154, 179
Church Militant, 162
Church Order, 153-158
Churches, The Younger, 156, 159
Churchism, 156-157
Clericalism, 48-49, 155, 157
Colossians, The Epistle to the, 81, 84, 117

211

INDEX

Communism, Marxist, 21-24, 47, 49, 63, 66, 102, 108, 148, 180
Community, The Historical, 123-130
Community, The Transcendental, 123-125, 128, 130
Congregations, 126-127
Corinthians, The Second Epistle to the, 85, 114, 124, 132, 138
Croall Lectures, 8

Damascus, 117
Davenport, 41
Death, 30, 89, 91-92, 173-174
Deissmann, Adolf, 97
Determinism, Economic, 49, 66
Devil, The, 28-32, 38, 169, 174
Diabolonians, The, 176
Disruption, The Great, 120
Dostoevski, F. M., 100, 174, 178
Dryden, John, 18
Dualism, 26

Ecumenical Movement, The, 129
Edinburgh, 8, 119
Einstein, Albert, 20
Election, Divine, 65-68, 92, 123
Eliot, T. S., 156
Enoch, Book of, 60
Ephesians, Epistle to the, Musical quality of, 17
Ephesus, 13
Epicurus, 75
Eros, 64
Evangelists, 145, 147
Evolution, 44, 63

Fasces, 21
Fatherhood of God, The, 56-57, 143
Fellowship of the Spirit, 11, 63
Form Criticism, 75
Frank, Erich, 38
Free-Masonry, 60
Freedom, Philosophy of, 45, 65-66
Fullness of Christ, The, 134, 160-164
Furies, The, 33

Galatians, The Epistle to the, 13, 15, 101, 103, 142
Gamaliel, 11, 18

Gentiles, 15-16, 40, 61, 71, 85, 91, 112-113, 160, 166, 168
Geopolitics, 49
Gnostics, 160
God-likeness, 97, 99, 169-170
Golgotha, 84, 91
Goodspeed, Edgar J., 17
Gospels, Synoptic, 58
Grand Inquisitor, The, 174

Hammer and Sickle, 21
Handel, George Frederick, 24
Harvard University, 46-47
Hebrews, The Epistle to the, 81, 86
Hedonism, 88, 189
Hegel, Georg Wilhelm Friedrich, 17, 74
Hinduism, 47, 103
Hispanidad, 48
Hocking, W. E., 47
Holy War, The, 104
Hope, Christian, 137
Hosea, 133
Hound of Heaven, The, 104
Humanity, The New, 61, 71-72, 142

Idealism, Absolute, 74
Imitation of God, The, 169ff.
Institutes of the Christian Religion, 67
Internationalism, 143
Islam, 47
Israel, The New, 61, 71, 125, 157

Japan, 41
Jeremiah, 41
Jerusalem, 70, 117, 124-125
Jews, 15-16, 40, 61, 71, 85, 91, 101, 108, 112-113, 160
John, St., 15, 150
John, The First Epistle of St., 15
John of the Cross, St., 19
Jordan River, 78, 80, 86, 89
Judaizers, 13-14, 160
Judas, 90
Justinian, 202

Kairos, 76
Kierkegaard, Soren, 178
Knox, John, 118
Kurios, 138

Law, The, 88, 90-91, 107
Laymen's Inquiry Concerning Christian Missions, A, 47
Lenin, Nikolay, 24, 180
Lewis, C S, 29, 31-32, 185
Lidgett, J. Scott, 14
Love, Everlasting and Invincible, 64ff.
Luke, St., 57
Luther, Martin, 24, 188

Mackinder, Sir Halford, 49
Man, The New, 71, 99ff., 135
Man, The Old, 35-36
Manchuria, 180
Mansoul, 104, 176
Mark, St., 57
Marx, Karl, 23-24, 63, 74
Materialism, 34, 49
Maynard, Sir John, 102
Milton, John, 30-34, 77, 81, 169
Mitton, C Leslie, 10n.
Moffatt, James, 41
Moralism, 88
Morbidity, 42
Moses, 12, 54, 70, 124
"Mystery," The, 2, 12, 52, 59-61, 64, 69, 82, 95-96, 139
Mystery Cults, 59
Myers, F. W. H, 102

Nazism, 95, 180
Nemesis, 33
Nihilism, 20-21, 41
Northrop, F S. C., 46

Objectivity, Scientific, 6
Occident, The, 41
Odeberg, Hugo, 27
Oikumene, 13
Orient, The, 41
Orthodoxy, Theological, 106
Oxford University, 31, 82-83

Palencia, The Christ of, 84
Panoply of God, The, 196
Paradise Lost, 30, 169
Paradise Regained, 77, 90
Pascal, Blaise, 106, 162
Pastors, 145, 148

Pentecostal Movement, The, 179-180
Percy, Ernst, 10n.
Pessimism, 20-21
Peter, St., 90, 130-131
Peter, The First Epistle of St., 15
Philippians, The Epistle to the, 81, 137, 173, 198
Phillips, J B, 150, 195-196
Pilgrim's Progress, The, 19, 104, 113-114, 116
Plato, 2, 44
Power, The Way of, 43, 47
Predestination, Divine, 65-68
Priesthood of Believers, The Universal, 151-152
Principalities and Powers, 22, 25, 32-34, 72, 84, 183, 186, 198
Prophets, New Testament, 145, 147
Protestantism, 128, 133, 178-179
Pythagoreans, 44

Rationalism, 23, 34
Reality, Ultimate, 56
Redemption, Divine, 103ff.
Rembrandt, 13
Republic, The, 2
Resurrection, of Christ, The, 91ff.
Rift, The Great, 25, 27, 32, 40, 43, 50, 61, 74, 122, 167-168
Robinson, J. Armitage, 27-28, 53
Romans, The Epistle to the, 15, 39, 53, 58, 108, 110, 125, 141
Rosenberg, Alfred, 108
de Rougemont, Denis, 29-30
Russia, 49-50, 102
Rutherford of Anworth, 133

Sacraments, The, 139, 156
Saint, Sainthood, 46, 52, 66-67, 102, 105, 107, 123, 149-154, 161, 166, 168, 175
Salvation, God's work of, 103ff, man's attempts to gain, 106ff.
Sartre, Jean-Paul, 100
Satan, 29-32, 80, 90, 176, 185, 196, 199
Schism, 136, 159
Schweitzer, Albert, 97
Scotland, The Church of, 119-121
Seeley, J R., 178
Septuagint, 58, 138

INDEX

Shield of Faith, 197
Simeon, Charles, 181
Sin, 30, 37, 43, 84, 87-91
Sisera, 33
Sodom, 39
Sorokin, Pitirim, 46
Spain's Golden Age, 48
Smith, G. A., 41
Stoics, 44, 171
Swastika, 21
Synge, F. C., 101

Teachers, 145, 148-149
Tennyson, Alfred, 124
Teresa of Ávila, 133
Theocracy, 48
Thompson, Francis, 33, 104
Toynbee, Arnold J, 36, 75-76, 178
Towards the Conversion of England, 147
Tritheism, 87

Truth, Personal, 166, 170, 172

Ulysses, 30
de Unamuno, Miguel, 84, 91, 100, 118, 178
Unity, Religious, 62-63, 139-141
Ur of the Chaldees, 55

Virgin Cult, The, 133
Virtue, The Way of, 107

Wells, H G., 94
Westminster Shorter Catechism, The, 37
Weymouth, Richard Francis, 150
Wheelwright, Philip, 3
Wisdom, The Way of, 43, 44
World Council of Churches, The, 140

Yale University, 46

www.ingramcontent.com/pod-product-compliance
Lightning Source LLC
Chambersburg PA
CBHW070251230426
43664CB00014B/2498